"Bruce continues to provide powerful c
for our organization. Our business ha
first time in 5 years! Highly recommend Bruce and The Sales Coaching
Group."

"Bruce has helped me achieve a disciplined organized approach to my business
development that has produced consistent results. His funnel management
and process techniques alone have greatly improved our ability to forecast and
hit our sales numbers.."

"Bruce Riggs is a natural born leader and an extraordinary salesperson. He's
very detail oriented, customer focused, personable, and very intelligent. Bruce
is a firm believer in following the sales process and earning the right with his
customers. This has made him very successful in his career. His motivation,
enthusiasm, and dedication are second to none. I'd recommend any sales
professional to learn from Bruce, he has a lot to offer!"

"Bruce is an exceptional coach, teacher and person. He's a motivational leader
who's information is timely. His dynamic approach and personality make it
easy to jump on board with the points he's communicating. I would
recommend Bruce wholeheartedly!"

"Bruce is a loyal advocate, teacher, and friend. He is the first "boss" that has
actually cared about my development, my family, and what I would like to
accomplish in my career. I would be much further along if I was provided the
opportunity to work with him early in my career."

"Bruce is the consummate sales professional and coach. He brings his vast
knowledge and cutting edge training techniques to our employees on a regular
basis. He is an outstanding executive and I'm happy to recommend the work
that he has done for our company."

I DIDN'T SIGN UP TO BE IN SALES

G . B R U C E R I G G S

A STEP-BY-STEP SALES PROCESS
FROM AMERICA'S BEST SMALL BUSINESS OWNERS

To order copies, book speaking, or signup for a
training workshop:

(918) 706-1992

bruce@bruceriggs.com

Written by:

G. Bruce Riggs, MBA

President

The Sales Coaching Group™

PERFORM ONE INSTITUTE ™

Tulsa, OK

Contact:

The Sales Coaching Group and / or PerformONE Training Group:

918 706-1992

bruce@bruceriggs.com

www.TheSalesCoachingGroup.com

www.PerformONEgroup.com

Table of Contents

Acknowledgments

Thank you to my wife, Tobi, and our children, Whitney, Austin, Alex, Bradleigh, and Nick who inspire me everyday to work harder and to keep pushing toward excellence. I am forever, grateful to God and his grace for such a wonderful family and encouraging wife.

My sincere thanks to my twin brother Brent, who continues to give and encourage. His creative genius and constant advice as a friend and partner have been invaluable. www.brentriggs.com

Thanks to my mother and father whose timely encouragement and support is always appreciated!

Thanks to my brother Kelly who introduced me to the joy of selling! www.vmaxpg.com

"Special thanks" to my editor Annie Kile. Anyone that works with Annie quickly discovers how passionate she is about business communication. I highly recommend her to anyone looking for an editor or strategic business partner.

www.bootstrap.business.development@gmail.com

Author

Glen Bruce Riggs, MBA

Bruce is the president of The Sales Coaching Group™ and PerformOne Training located in Tulsa, Oklahoma. He serves as a consultant and performance coach in the area of sales, sales management, and business development. Bruce also sits on the advisory board for several organizations.

Bruce has a diverse and highly successful background in sales and executive leadership in companies ranging in size from startup to the Fortune 100 level, including national award and multiple performance records as a Sales Management Executive.

Along with his MBA, Bruce has completed post-academic work at the renowned Tepper School of Business (Carnegie Mellon University), and is currently a highly acclaimed adjunct professor.

Bruce is married and the father of 3 children. For more information, visit www.PerformONEgroup.com.

Editor

Annie Kile

Ask anyone who knows her, and they'll tell you that Annie Kile is a communicator – and communication is the most powerful transaction that takes place in any business. Annie is highly recommended and respected for her collaboration and business consultation.

Annie can be contacted at:

bootstrap.business.development@gmail.com.

Introduction

Trust.

Firm reliance on the integrity, ability, or character of a person or thing.

Custody; care.

Something committed into the care of another; charge.

Confidence; the condition and resulting obligation of having confidence placed in one.

Reliance on something in the future; hope.

The first thing that comes to mind as I put this introduction together is to say that the process of reading this book mirrors the process of trust-based selling this book is all about. Every chapter is written with the goal of building the trust of my readers.

Many of you are reading this book because you want to learn how America's best business owners and top sales performers are growing their companies year after year. However, many of you (Business Owners, CEOs, Presidents), have informed me, "I didn't sign up to be in sales." Well, nothing happens in business until a sale is made. You are "officially" your company's Chief Sales Officer. Top business performers know you only stay on top by making continuous improvement a part of your process.

We're going to talk a lot about process and a lot about trust because trust is the foundation upon which successful business is built. The behaviors and activities that build trust are also a process, and a process is something that can be taught and duplicated over and over again. This book will teach you those processes in ways that can be immediately applied.

What drove me to write this book was my desire and mission to put 25 years and at least 50,000 hours of sales and sales management experience to work for you. By "you" I mean both business owners as well as front line sales leaders. This book is especially useful for business owners who find themselves (and often times rather unexpectedly) either managing a sales force or selling themselves (sometimes both) without any experience or training to back them up.

In today's highly competitive markets, a company's greatest competitive advantage are individuals who have the ability to develop rock solid business relationships built on competence, integrity, compassion and, most of all - trust. The best sales organizations also demonstrate keen skill in communicating competitive advantages as well as planning and understanding the power of process.

For a variety of reasons, many business-development professionals are not provided the level of training that will truly benefit the company and significantly increase individual performance. Furthermore, often due to necessity, many sales managers are promoted based on past sales performance and do not have the skills or training to effectively coach their business-development teams.

I've already noted that a central concept of this book is process. This book will assist you in meeting (and exceeding) your goals and the goals of your company by sharing a specific process designed to produce high performance sales teams and individuals. The first step in that process is to identify traits common to top performers. The top 5% performers tend to exhibit common traits:

- They are disciplined

- They are lifelong learners

- They are process-oriented

- They have the ability to effectively identify and communicate competitive advantages

The second step is learning, practicing, and continuously improving specific key sales processes; processes that meet the requirements of being both replicable and measurable. For sales managers this means being able to teach as well as train teams in these processes. A key benefit of process is that is has a built-in major sales success factor: Accountability. Providing members of the sales team with the ongoing support they need develops habitual adherence to process and, in turn, accountability.

The benefit for individual sales professionals reading this book is twofold. First and foremost, you can immediately apply the concepts and processes as the most effective means to achieve your individual goals and objectives, not to mention exceed goals set by your organization. Second, individual sales professionals are always a part of a team and bringing back to your company and colleagues what you learn in this book is a major contribution to the success of your company. Even if you are the sole person whose job description is to sell, each and every person working for your organization is a part of your team and contributes to winning the sale.

Over the years I have been privy time and time again to witness how a disciplined sales process leads to consistent performance excellence. However, I have also been amazed to find that very few sales professionals can tell you what process they follow that consistently produces success as opposed to process they followed that consistently failed to win the sale. Instead, too many "average" salespeople shoot from the hip which provides an equally average rate when it comes to hitting the target.

The ability to measure and produce replicable results cannot be emphasized enough. In our Sales Process PLUS++ (ADVISED) process, we do three key things:

- Get Information

- Give Information

- Get Commitment

Those of you committed to continuously educating yourself in order to improve your skills might note this is the formula taught by the Miller/Heinman Performance Company. In my organizations, The Sales Coaching Group, and PerformONE Training, we have modified this process to emphasize some additional key development areas that are crucial to replicable sales performance - areas that you will learn about in this book which, when put into practice, provide continuous improvement year after year.

One very important aspect of any sales environment is the culture a sales team operates. I have been associated with great sales teams; startup and Fortune 100 teams; and, unfortunately, dysfunctional sales teams. In almost every case, we were fortunate to have truly outstanding product and service offering.

Despite having the most competitive offering, one particular team consistently underperformed in sales as well as suffered a high turnover rate. Those who remained represented a resentful, sullen, and demotivated regional sales force whose goals and objectives seemed to be sabotaging just about everything the company was trying to achieve.

In contrast, during a six-year period starting in the early 2000's, a highly effective team achieved better than 30%+ growth for several years running. The morale of the team was very high, and turnover was nonexistent.

What was the difference?

The high performance team developed a process-oriented culture founded on trust-based selling and invested in the training and development of the entire sales development team. It is critical for leaders in the professional office to develop their professional sales staff to win new customers. Sales Process++ eliminates the chaos of underachieving or dysfunctional sales teams and this book introduces key concepts of our highly successful sales process that can be put into place immediately.

Goals:

- Develop a High Performance Culture – create a disciplined sales organization that produces consistent results. Focus on hiring, training and developing sales skills that mimic the Top 5%. High

Performance sales organizations have a strong awareness of the importance of trust.

- Defend Your Best Customers – 20% of your customers produce 80% of your revenue. Leverage your customer service as a strategic advantage.

- Communicate Your Competitive Advantages – competitive advantages are why you are in business. Effective application of a sales process requires a keen understanding of what makes you different.

- Develop a Sales Process – a disciplined sales process provides clarity and focus. It allows for consistency, replication and natural accountability.

- Plan Strategically – the best sales organizations today plan to win.

TRUST

"I trust you."

These are hardly the words that usually come to mind when struggling to meet sales goals. However, these three simple words should be the goal for every communication between sales professionals and their customers – because business is developed not by making sales, but by building trust. Trust is the transaction, trust is the exchange, and trust is the result of building relationships of mutual reciprocity.

True relationships of mutual reciprocity are not of the "I'll scratch your back, you'll scratch mine" variety. A true reciprocal relationship is one of balance, with neither party attempting to dominate or "win." Instead, in reciprocal relationships both parties understand that the relationship is one of mutual *dependence,* and when we depend on someone, trust in that person is absolutely essential.

It is safe to say, and our research supports, that the top 5% of sales professionals in the domestic United States build their book of business on trust. As a matter-of-fact, trust is the one skill that sales people can improve that will have an immediate, positive, and measurable impact on their bottom line. However, before one can improve a skill, one must have an understanding of exactly what that skill is, and this begs the question:

What is this thing called trust?

Anyone seeking an "absolute" definition of trust will be sorely disappointed. Even academics seeking to research trust have cited the problem of not having a universally accepted definition of trust. Most dictionaries refer to

> "Only a foundation of trust results in collaboration and goodwill necessary to achieve peak performance"
>
> Roger K. Allen

trust as a "belief" about a person. We "trust" someone is being honest with us can easily be rewritten as we "believe" someone is being honest with us. It follows that, when developing skills related to establishing trust, we are actually trying to develop the skills needed to get people to *believe* in us.

But, just what is it that we want people to believe about us as sales professionals? We want people to believe we have their best interests at heart. We want people to believe in our ability to provide solutions that work to solve *their* problems and the products or services that meet *their* needs. When our customers believe in us, trust us, they are more than willing to make a purchase. Why? Because people will buy based on their hearts and justify that purchase based on logic.

When I say people buy based on their hearts what I mean is people buy based on belief, and belief is a subjective feeling. In other words, belief is emotionally based. However, people are also rational beings. We act on emotion but rationalize the validity of our emotions using logic. We reason things out based on both facts and inferences.

Most of us are familiar with the logical reasoning in the statement "If A equals B, and B equals C, then C equals A." It only makes sense for this to be true, it is a logical assumption. Again, it might appear to be a quantum leap in thought to apply logical reasoning to the idea that trust is the foundation for successful business development – so let's take a stab at creating a logical statement regarding the power of trust in sales:

"I trust (A) Salesperson Bob (B). Bob sells something I need (C). Therefore, I trust (A) that this purchase from Bob (B) is the right thing to do."

Trust (A) = Bob (B)

Bob (B) = Fulfilled Need (C)

Fulfilled Need (C) = Trust (A)

Well, it isn't a perfectly logical statement, but, if you go ahead and plug the A, B, and C found in our "sales logic" statement into the mathematical expression you can see that because Bob is

 trusted and Bob can fill a need, the customer can logically infer they can trust they've made a good decision buying from Bob. Just as important, we can also deduce that it is only logical for sales professionals to identify trust as the foundation for successful business development – but we still have that sticky problem establishing some sort of definition of trust.

What Trust is Not

Because trust is such a difficult thing to define, understanding what trust *isn't* goes a long way to being able to identify what trust is.

Many of us view trust akin to a personality trait. There is "something" about a person that engenders our willingness to trust them. But trust is **not** a personality trait that people are born with. Instead, trust, or trustworthiness, is something that develops as a part of our essential character. Too often we confuse personality traits to be as static and unchanging as the physical traits we are born with. We're born and will reach a certain height as an adult and nothing is going to change that. We have long fingers or short fingers and nothing is going to change that. We're born with a particular personality that makes it easy for people to trust us or we're not – right?

Wrong. While one of the things that make this world such a wonderful and interesting place is the fact that we get to experience and know people with different personalities, personality traits are *not* the substance of personal character. Personal character is formed and developed over our lifetimes. Our character, our values, and our behaviors are not static, instead personal character is a dynamic factor of being human. Most important is that we have control over and can develop our character.

And personal character isn't a singular attribute – rather it is a grouping of a variety of characteristics. And it is a grouping of particular characteristics that render a person worthy of another's trust. Furthermore, this grouping of trustworthy personal characteristics, taken together as a whole, is what people will use to base both their "from the heart" as well as "logical" perception that you are someone they can trust to develop the relationship of mutual reciprocity necessary for successful, profitable business development.

How Trust Operates

So far we've been talking about what trust is and isn't in subjective terms - but what does trust look like in the real world? Rather than simply jumping in and giving you a laundry list – let's first take a look at how trust operates in society in general.

Trust plays a significant role when it comes to serving our most basic human need – survival. If we are to survive, a primary goal is to create a secure and safe environment. One-way humans have found to be of great assistance when it comes to survival is living together in collaborative groups.

> "I know in my heart that man is good. That what is right will always eventually triumph. And there's purpose and worth to each and every life."
>
> **Ronald Reagan**

Because humans are social beings, creating a safe, secure environment depends a lot on being able to predict what others will do. When our ancestors went out to hunt in groups they needed to trust that the bounty would be shared. Add to this scenario the fact that humans don't want to simply "survive", we have an inborn urge to thrive and progress. We constantly seek to improve the quality of our lives and, in order to do that, we need to associate with those we can trust to support or contribute to our best interests as well as their own.

Since our goal is to survive and improve the conditions we live in, the ability to predict the behavior of others is central to our success. We need to be able to identify those we can trust (predict) will support and/or contribute to our efforts in a way that benefits us.

How we do that is to look for a grouping of characteristics that indicate a person (or a thing, such as a product and/or service we sell) is worthy of our trust – and this is exactly how a prospective customer or client qualifies who they will trust their business to.

The Great Communicator

We've discussed what trust isn't and, while we still don't have an absolute definition for trust, we've established that trust is critical to our ability to survive and thrive because it allows us to predict how others will behave towards us. We know that we identify trust by specific characteristics – now let's take a look at some of those characteristics.

An excellent example of someone who embodied characteristics of trust is Ronald Reagan. President Reagan took office in tumultuous and uncertain times. People felt insecure as to both our nation's security as well as their own survival. The country had just brought home hostages who had been held for 444 days in Iran. The Cold War wasn't something in books or movies – it was a political reality. The economy was experiencing a severe recession. Filling your gas tank meant waiting in long lines, sometimes for hours.

Somehow, despite all the turmoil, even those who did not fully support his policies came to call President Reagan "The Great Communicator." However, it wasn't solely his skill as a public speaker that rallied the country, it was what he communicated – Reagan communicated trust. To this day Reagan's status as a trusted leader remains intact. In the last 12 years, including 2011, a Gallop poll reported Americans touting Reagan as the "greatest United States President." In 2000, the Wall Street Journal surveyed over 100 academicians asking them to rank historical presidencies. Reagan took eighth place out of a possible forty-three.

Just how did Reagan communicate his trustworthiness so successfully? Simple, he demonstrated a group of characteristics that are indicative of trust. For one, Reagan was known for his kindness and as a man who based his actions on a sincere love for humanity. For example, we all know that Reagan survived being shot during in an assassination attempt. What many people don't know is that during his hospitalization, Reagan noticed water had spilled onto the floor. When his aides came into the room they found the President on his knees wiping it up, turned out he was concerned a nurse or other employee might get into trouble. Remember, this is a 70 year old man who, just days earlier, had been shot in the chest causing him to lose 40-50% of his blood volume – not to mention he was the President of the United States.

What this story demonstrates is that trust happens when a person is oriented to the world in such a way that one's personal experience is not the sole motivation when taking action. Trust happens when we behave in ways that communicate to others that we recognize their experience, their needs, their problems, their hopes, their dreams, their fears, to be just as real to that person as our own experience and perspective is to us.

Reagan also valued optimism and translated that optimism into a clear and positive vision for our nation. This optimistic, positive view of our nation created trust on the part of the American people, as well as the world, that America's ideals of freedom and liberty were safe now and would continue to be safe in the future.

Reagan communicated his great optimism and vision when he reminded us "America is too great for small dreams." And, while he was the President who coined the term "Evil Empire" when referring to the former Soviet Union, at the same time Reagan communicated to Soviet leadership a willingness to be open and flexible. This openness infers intimacy, and intimacy requires being both transparent (as opposed to manipulative) and flexible when communicating with others.   Open, transparent, and flexible communications create trust.   In his case, Reagan's ability to communicate trust with Soviet leaders resulted in the deconstruction of the Berlin wall as well as the ability to negotiate with the U.S.S.R. for peaceful relations as partners instead of adversaries.

The Responsibility Factor

Reagan, of course, was interested in building a better America. Most sales professionals aren't interested in becoming President of the United States, but all of us in sales are interested in building business.   And we can learn a lot about what characterizes trust – the trust that builds business - from Reagan. His words, and the actions that accompanied those words, displayed key elements of trust. Reagan built trust because he deeply understood, and freely accepted, he was responsible for managing our country in ways that served the well being of the American people. Similarly, sales professionals are responsible for the well being of their customers and clients.

The idea that the professional sales person is responsible for the well being of their customer may sound rather radical. Too often, sales professionals see their primary responsibility to be making their goals. Sure, every sales person worth their salt knows that networking and creating relationships is integral to closing sales. However, all too few understand that it is the *quality* of these relationships that close sales – and, once again, relationships based on trust are quality relationships.

For example, one characteristic that a customer looks for when seeking a salesperson they can trust is expertise. We are living in an age where customers have easy access to information when researching and investigating during the buying decision cycle, so it would seem logical that the sales person's level of expertise would diminish in importance. However, what is interesting is that our now vastly better informed potential (and current) customers expect the salesperson to be much more informed than they are. Customers hold the salesperson responsible to act as their expert advisor while making their buying decision – and place their trust in sales professionals who, like Reagan, freely accept and deeply understand their responsibility for the well-being of their customer.

This whole idea of being responsible for the well being of your customers might be better understood if we use the legal definition of the word "trust." When used in the legal sense of the term, the basic definition of a trust is an arrangement where a person (trustor) gives fiduciary control over something of value (money, property) to another person (trustee). Quite often, a trustee is expected to *manage* the trust and, this management must always be in the best interest of the trustor, not the trustee.

In a very real sense a customer gives a salesperson fiduciary control over something of value, after all making a purchase involves the exchange of money (or other property). However, before they make the purchase, the customer expects that the salesperson to act in ways that serve *the customer's* interest (well-being). In other words, customers are looking for a fiduciary relationship with a sales professional. Interestingly enough, the word "fiduciary" comes from the Latin word for, you guessed it, "trust."

And, just as trustee's are often responsible to manage the money or property the trustor has given them, customers expect sales professionals to manage both the "pre" and "post" purchase process – again, in a manner that serves the customer's best interest.

[1]Trust Formula =

$$\frac{E2 + D + R}{SO}$$

E2=Experience & Expertise

D= Dependability

R=Rapport

SO=Self-Orientation

The principle of the Trust Formula is adopted from the work of Mr. David Maister in his book "The Trusted Advisor. (Maister, 1997)

I have changed the formula terms to suit our intent.

Trust is a very difficult word to define. A formula provides clarity of the four elements and how one can improve their ability to develop trust with a potential or current customer.

Post Chapter Exercise:

1. List 5 things you have accomplished this year to develop greater expertise.

2. What could you do immediately to improve your client or customer's perception of your dependability?

3. What is built into your sales process regarding building rapport or long-term relationship with your clients?

4. Pull your last 6 emails. Count how many times you used the words "I" or "me." Rewrite the emails. Exchange "I" and "me" with "you" or "yours."

CHARACTER

In most professional offices, 80 percent of the business is developed by 20 percent of the firm's employees. Sound familiar? Yes, it is Pareto's Law at work. In the early 1900's, Italian economist Vilfredo Pareto used this equation to describe the unequal distribution of wealth in his country, observing that 20 percent of the population owned 80 percent of the wealth. This formula was later given a broader business application by Dr. Joseph M. Juran, and Pareto's Principle (also called Pareto's Law) became a very worthy tool for effective management.

What are the common characteristics of these high achievers?

1. Passion
2. Attitude
3. Competitiveness

Passion

The most successful professionals are those who train hard, learn the science, and have "passion" for developing new business. I

am often asked what I believe is the most important
characteristic of a
"high achiever."
Undoubtedly,
there are a number
of important skills
and talents
exhibited by great

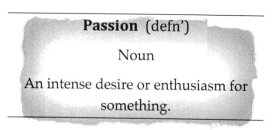

Passion (defn')

Noun

An intense desire or enthusiasm for something.

business developers, but the one key element that is common to
all the ones I have coached is *passion*. I read a blog about a
business owner who judges passion with his simple "Monday
Test." He explained that if a "partner" consistently wakes up on
Monday morning dreading to go to work, he or she is definitely
in the wrong job.

Passion, I think, is rooted in belief:

You believe that you are a great employee.
You believe that you work for a great company.
You believe that you are selling the best product or services.

If you do not believe those three statements, you are in the
wrong industry, the wrong company, or, worse still, the wrong
job. These three beliefs are the foundation for the passion that
creates high performance. Are you passionate about developing

new business? Are you passionate about the product or service you are selling? In my estimation, passion is absolutely critical for top business professionals. *In fact, mediocrity stems more from a lack of belief than a lack of skill.*

Anders Ericsson, a psychologist at Florida State University, conducted research into how superior performers are able to excel at what they do, and he reached two significant conclusions. First, the top performer is motivated by his or her passion. Second, the top performer is driven to practice his or her skills rigorously.

> *"Deliberate practice drives expert performance. Passion provides the motivation necessary to practice rigorously."*

Top performers are able to practice long and hard, and apply themselves more intensely than average performers, precisely because they are doing something that they love to do. If you do not love what you do, chances are good that you will never put in the time needed to master it.

Following battle wounds suffered in Iraq in 2007, Corporal Garrett Jones lost one of his legs. Following the amputation, he told his doctors that he hoped to do two things - have a family, and return to snowboarding. Unfortunately, while having a family would be no problem, doctors thought it unlikely that the above-knee amputee would be able to snowboard. Jones, apparently, was unconvinced.

Two years later, Jones is spinning 360s and boosting big airs at Timberline Ski Area, thanks to an Oregon entrepreneur's perseverance and a unique prosthetic knee. Jones's passion for snowboarding helped him overcome impossible odds. "The first time out, my leg fell off," he said. Duct tape fixed that.

Are we not inspired by this story? A combat hero who refuses to let misfortune and disfigurement prevent him from participating in something he loves? Passion is what creates a refuse-to-fail mentality that overcomes the most significant obstacles.

It is passion that also compels salespeople to communicate the benefits of their products and services with total conviction and belief. It is passion that allows salespeople to really care and listen to the concerns of their customers. In fact, it is passion that drives salespeople to overcome any challenge or hurdle.

If you have not uncovered your "passion in life," it may be time to try a new approach. Here are three easy steps to work on developing "passion":

Consider your true passion

Passion usually develops out of an interest in something specific. What are your current interests? What is it that really captures your imagination? For example, if you discovered that a loved one had a hearing deficiency, could you possibly develop a passion for selling hearing instruments? My point is that there is always something in our lives we are passionate about.

Develop, train, and nurture your passion

Nurture the interests you have identified. Research them and learn everything you can. One of two things is likely to happen - the foundation is laid and your interest continues to grow, or your interest fades and you can "cross it off" your list of potential passions.

Find a coach or mentor

Identify people you think are passionate about your interests. Learn something about them and ask them to share their ideas about their passions. Ask them why they are excited. Specifically, learn about how their passion(s) developed. I have been fortunate to have several mentors, and my experience is that you can learn by watching and listening.

Attitude

Sometime during Alexander the Great's early formative years, he decided to model himself after the Greek mythological hero Achilles. Olympias, Alexander's mother,

> **Attitude** (defn')
>
> Noun
>
> The way a person views something or tends to behave towards it.

encouraged this; and apparently his teacher, the great philosopher Aristotle, did so as well. In keeping with the expectations of his mother, Alexander looked for any opportunity to demonstrate his heroic strength, courage, and conquering attitude. Ultimately, the power of Alexander's attitude and his charismatic personality changed the world.

A great attitude cannot be overlooked as the foundation of a great career. All the top business-development professionals I have worked with and had the privilege to train have demonstrated a great attitude in front of customers, with their managers, and to their peers. In my opinion, one of the secrets of a great salesperson is what goes on inside their head.

"I would rather live a short life of glory than a long one of obscurity." - Alexander the Great

Great business leaders first uncover attitude tendencies during the interview process. Typically, interviews are designed to help employers get to know candidates better and establish whether a candidate responds well to questions regarding the duties and expectations of the job. While the candidate that performs best during the interview may be the clear winner of the interview process, there is little data to support that the best-performing candidate during interviews will prove to be the best candidate for the job. However, questions designed to reveal internal attitudes are excellent indicators of a candidate's potential to excel in sales.

One of my best hires was an Air Force Captain and a graduate of the Citadel Military Academy. (Bryan Studebaker, US Air Force, Security Forces) The men and women at the academy live and study under a classical military system that makes leadership and character training an essential part of the educational experience. I was immediately impressed with Bryan's great attitude and asked him to join our team. His first year on the team proved to be highly successful as he learned our industry, products, and customers much quicker than other new hires. The difference? A strong desire to succeed coupled with a great attitude toward work.

Research produced by The HR Chally Group indicates that, more often than not, the motivation and attitude one brings to a specific job influences success more than skills. Specific job skills can be taught, but attitudes and motivation are intrinsic to an individual's core beliefs, and are the key drivers of performance.

In order to develop highly productive attitudes, employees involved in business development should:

Move away from energy-draining people.

Have you ever been naturally drawn to a great leader? Conversely, are there people you would duck into a room to avoid? The people we hide from usually have negative or critical attitudes that sap our energy; they seem to wear a type of people repellent! People with great attitudes, on the other hand, are fun to be around, and often attract raises, promotions, and success. Surround yourself with people that have great attitudes.

Learn to be happy!

I know this may sound trite, but choosing to be happy has a

positive correlation on good attitude. When you are having a really "bad attitude" day, find something to be happy about. Despite our circumstances, happiness is a choice, something addressed in detail by Steven Covey in his bestseller *The 7 Habits of Highly Effective People.* Physiologically, choosing to be happy rather than reacting negatively will help to ease tension and enhance your ability to influence and persuade.

Change your perception

You can take two different people from the same exact situation and each of them can have a different attitude. Attitude is about perception. Notice the people you work with. Some love Mondays while others think "Monday" is a bad word. . Change your perception and you change your attitude.

Above all else, success in selling is about attitude! It is how you think and feel. It is about your whole approach to yourself, your company, your products, and your customers.

Competitiveness

"There's nothing that cleanses your soul like getting the hell kicked out of you." – Coach Woody Hayes

I admire Woody Hayes. Unfortunately, he was a hot-tempered, difficult, and aggressive man at times. He was also loving, gentle, and a father-like figure to many young men and coaches. I

Competitive (defn')

Adjective

A strong desire to be more successful than others.

laugh out loud when I read Lou Holtz's autobiography and his discussion of Woody Hayes. In Lou's book, he tells the story of how Woody fired him six times "unofficially." Usually, it was over something that Woody did not understand or take the time to get all the facts.

Why did Lou love Woody? Much of Lou's life was a contradiction of personality compared to Coach Hayes. A multitude of people have different opinions of Woody, but no one would disagree on one thing: he absolutely refused to lose. Woody was difficult to understand, but those who knew him privately understood that competing was everything to him. In the end, players and coaches were extremely loyal and dedicated to him.

Like Coach Hayes, top employees refuse to lose. Built into their "being" is the desire to compete and win. Successful professional people seem to compete at everything! Cards, sports, sales quota, or the quickest to score during a sales contest--everything! For truly great sales professionals, there is a burning desire for recognition and achievement. It is very important for sales managers to learn how to manage these high achievers. Competing and winning is a primary motivation. Why?

For some people, there is a primal instinct that compels them to achieve; that drive is behind each thought and action. To these people, money is a secondary motivation. Respect and their impact on their organization are higher motivators. Competition and winning plays a vital and important role in becoming fully satisfied and content with our life's ambition. Competition and achievement sets a legacy. A life full of personal wins further build upon each success to the point where winning becomes the norm rather than the exception. Part of our legacy is to leave one that we can look back on with pride at the end of a career and know that we embraced all our opportunities to the fullest.

Woody Hayes certainly has left a legacy.

(*Story out of the Ohio State Archives*)-"One time after practice, where Woody would always ride the first bus out while the team caught the second bus, the first bus left without Woody, and he was enraged. He threw his briefcase in the middle of the parking lot and it split open and play sheets flew everywhere. Woody then hopped on the second bus and the bus driver took off in an effort to catch the first bus. Assistant Lou McCullough recalled, "It was the first time in history that a vehicle of any kind -- let alone a bus -- ever careened through campus at 75 miles an hour, with Woody bellowing every foot of the way. Woody just would not be upstaged, and the driver knew his life wasn't safe if he didn't overtake that first bus." Woody refused to lose.

I have always appreciated that you can challenge competitive professionals to do great things. In 2006, I managed a group of strategic account managers for a medical imaging company. Two thousand six had been challenging. Competitors had begun to copy our tactics and implement several of the strategies that we had been beating them with. Strategically, changes were needed going into next year, however there was still an urgency about finishing 2006. Expectations were high for our Strategic Business Unit ("SBU"). The SBU averaged greater than 30% growth for the past four years and was expected to finish strong again!

The SBU scheduled a strategic planning session in October to evaluate our plan and work toward a strong finish. It was decided to implement a competition during the three months of the fourth quarter. This was a new tactic. Previously, the SBU had exceeded expectations without sales contests. Our position within the industry was one of leadership. We were not sure a sales contest would produce significant increases. We were wrong.

Fortunately, the team responded enthusiastically to the contest and far exceeded expectations in October. We challenged the team again during November, this time asking for an all-time monthly sales record to be broken. The team competed against their own performance criteria and was rewarded and recognized for achieving against their own goals. The result was awesome.

In two short months, we stopped worrying about growth and now focused on achieving something truly spectacular. We set stretch goals that would have the SBU exceeding 40% growth over last year to date.

We achieved our 40% growth and were reminded about the power and benefit of competition. Great sales people love to compete; and when challenged, nurtured, and encouraged, will truly perform the spectacular. The year ended as one of the most rewarding and exhilarating of my career.

Many lessons can be learned from 2006, none more profound than the belief in hiring "competitive" individuals, developing their technical skills, and then getting out of their way! Many sales books proclaim the importance of money motivation and past experience as indicators to hiring successful salespeople. Although there may be some importance in looking for those elements, I strongly advocate testing for competitiveness, investing in great sales training, and letting them run.

In business development, there are no rewards for second place.

This trend of intensifying competition makes selling more interesting - but also much more difficult than it once was. You cannot assume you will remain successful simply by doing the same things that used to work for you.

Stop losing sales to competition. Start making more money by sharpening your competitive-selling skills. Here are four of the most common reasons why competitive salespeople lead their organizations:

They know their competitive advantages.

In his classic book, *The Art of War,* written 2,500 years ago, Sun Tzu wrote "If you know not yourself, you will lose every battle." The point is: what makes you better? It is critical to take time to understand this question. It will make your "initial benefit statement" and "closing the opportunity" much more powerful.

Chapter Exercise:

Learn your "true" competitive advantages. No one cares that you have great service and great products. We all do! It is the price of doing business.

Competitive salespeople defeat call reluctance and "fish where the fish are."

Competitive salespeople will knock down any door to provide a good solution to a customer need. All decision makers are not created equal. In every buying decision, there exists a person who can make things happen. Great salespeople are determined to get to this level of decision maker. Perhaps it is a VP or CFO or even the CEO. Too many salespeople are happy to go through the same monotonous exercise of begging a purchasing agent to speak with you. Great competitive salespeople learn the underpinnings of business and go talk business with business people.

Chapter Exercise:

Go call on someone that can make a decision. I see much bureaucracy in organizations today. Typically, this is a byproduct of poor leadership and can bog down our ability to sell solutions. To win, go see people who can make a decision or influence a decision. Stop walking in the same path that a hundred other average sales representatives have beat down.

Competitive salespeople learn a Sales Process and practice.

How do you measure where you are at in a sales call? What do you do if something unexpected happens? Why do some salespeople seem to close every deal without the gimmicks? The answer is a formalized sales process that helps you to understand where you are at every junction in the sales call. Successful salespeople do not take anything for granted. They develop a formalized process that is replicable and leads to winning more consistently than those salespeople who do not take the time to learn great processes.

Chapter Exercise:

Stop relying on your company to "spoon-feed" you everything. Do you have a self-awareness of your training needs? Do you have a formalized sales process or strategic-questioning skills? If not, find a sales coach and learn your profession.

Great salespeople have a plan to beat the competition.

The days of salespeople thinking they are fast enough to think on their feet and be successful are over. Selling has become more complex as buyers have become more educated concerning our products and services. The bias for quick thinking and a high activity level is exactly the opposite of what it takes to win competitive sales. I always love to compete against those individuals that think they are a natural and do not plan their sale. Fact is--we beat them 100% of the time. I am not suggesting you make fewer sales calls. What I am saying is that you need to put more thought into each call you make. Think like a coach thinks, and make a game plan to win. What is your understanding of your prospect's buying criteria? Which of those criteria represent a competitive advantage for you? Which represent a competitive disadvantage? How can you influence the customer's buying criteria in such as way as to create a better match between what you have and what your customer needs? Have you effectively produced a set of strategic questions?

Chapter Exercise:

The top 5% of salespeople have a plan. This is truly the #1 area that needs attention by average salespeople. Do you know how many customers it takes to achieve your goals? Do you know what your product mix needs to be? Do you know your daily, weekly, and monthly targets that guarantee success? Again, if you have never been taught the skill of developing a plan that is replicable and measurable and leads to success year after year, you need to get a sales coach to help you learn this critical skill.

COMPETITIVE ADVANTAGES

Walmart Wins

No matter what products your company sells, no matter what services your company may provide, when you compete on price the game is over because "Walmart *always* wins."

Price is never a competitive advantage unless your intent is to use this strategy as a means to erode your profit margin to the point where closing your doors is a distinct possibility. Just ask Kmart.

While a certain amount of retail conceit surely contributed to their demise as the number one discount big box retailer, when push came to shove in 2001 and they decided to take on that gorilla in the living room they made the mistake of deciding to compete on price with Walmart. With disastrous results. In January of 2002 Kmart filed for bankruptcy and has been struggling ever since.

It is time to stop struggling to compete and instead leverage your competitive advantages. Because your goal isn't to struggle – your goal is to win.

The Big Three

When Janie L. Smith put her book "Creating Competitive Advantage" together she asked a thousand CEOs to describe their company's competitive advantage. Only two were able to provide a definitive response. The remaining 998 chimed in by providing what, for many of us, are the "usual suspects" when it comes to describing our company's competitive advantage:

1. Price (no surprise there).

2. Quality of product

3. Level of customer service

None of the above, in and of themselves, can be cited as competitive advantages.

This may sound like a pretty radical statement. Don't customers want quality products at low prices delivered via superior customer service? The answer is, of course, "Yes." As a matter of fact, the customer question your competitive advantages must be able to answer is:

"Why should I buy from you?"

Clearly it isn't enough to respond to tell your customer "I've got a great price on quality product and we deliver great customer service." Any, we can go so far as to say *every*, sales person in the world has that response up their sleeve. Of course your company delivers on The Big Three; the challenge is to identify what it is about *how* you apply and implement The Big Three that separates you from the pack.

Of course there is always the temptation to try and differentiate by focusing on tightly knit niche markets. But selling to a "different" market does not differentiate your company because any niche market comes with competitors for that market. Customers in that market still ask the same question, "Why should I buy from you?"

You're right back where you started from.

The Rules

Most of us have been chasing the tail of The Big Three proudly touting them off to customers and clients as the reason they should buy from us. But simply parroting The Big Three doesn't make them a competitive advantage. Obviously you will always be competing on price, quality, and service.

If The Big Three aren't competitive advantages – what are they? In and of themselves, they are simply the base price of doing business.

However, if we follow some pretty simple rules, The Big Three can help identify exactly the unique competitive advantages that differentiate us from the pack that compel our customers to buy. What are these rules?

1. A competitive advantage is quantifiable

2. A competitive advantage can be proved

3. A competitive advantage cannot be easily duplicated

Following these three simple rules requires work – but doing the work reaps great returns – and, when done right, these returns are garnered quickly and at high rates. Applying these rules put the advantage back into focusing on the competitive advantages of your business. Following the rules can:

• Dramatically increase closing ratio

- Significantly boost margin

- Substantially increase market share

- Considerably increase market share

Another advantage of following the rules is they keep you from swimming around in circles by making common mistakes even good companies are guilty of:

- Think they're leveraging competitive advantage when they aren't even close

- Count on lowering price rather than using true competitive advantages

- Identify true competitive advantages but don't communicate them to prospects or customers

- Mistake strengths for competitive advantages

- Don't focus on competitive advantages when making strategic decisions

What You See is What You Get

" Truly great companies understand the difference between what should never change and what should be open for change, between what is

genuinely sacred and what is not. This rare ability to manage continuity and change — requiring a consciously practiced discipline — is closely linked to the ability to develop a vision." James C. Collins and Jerry I. Porras

Attempting to create or identify competitive advantages – never mind leverage those advantages – is putting the cart before the horse. You can identify competitive advantages that follow The Rules to the letter of the law – but first a company must have a compelling vision because it is a company's vision that drives innovative competitive advantage.

A company's vision leads that company into the future. Surely there is no crystal ball – but a company's vision paints a vivid picture that describes what your company would look like in its "most perfect" future. A company's vision articulates purpose and fuels passion. But a company's vision isn't some sort of magic pixie dust sprinkled on your website. Your company's vision isn't a tag line. A company's vision must commit and inspire, whether CEO or production line worker, to do the work necessary to translate the "future perfect" state described in your vision a reality.

When done correctly, a company's vision guides every business strategy – *including strategy to leverage competitive advantage.*

Take Apple for example. It is obvious that Apple is a visionary company with visionary leadership. Volumes can, and have, been written about Apple, especially about a man who many consider this century's most visionary business leader – Apple cofounder and CEO Steve Jobs.

Yet Apple's short vision statement alone makes it easy to see the connection between vision, strategy, and competitive advantage:

"Apple is committed to bringing the best personal computing experience to students, educators, creative professionals and consumers around the world through its innovative hardware, software and Internet offerings."

In their book "Built to Last: Successful Habits of Visionary Companies" James C. Collins and Jerry I. Porras describe a "well-conceived" vision statement as consisting of two parts: core ideology and envisioned future. The core ideology of a company is that company's "enduring character" that "transcends" internal or external changes; whereas the "envisioned future" describes what the company desires to become, the extreme aspirations a company wishes to achieve.

These two components work hand in hand and both must be present in order for a company's vision to continuously function in the context of creating its most perfect state – no matter what changes may occur. Many companies are now struggling in our current economic milieu due more to uncertain company ideology than economic uncertainty. When companies have a vision that clearly defines their core ideology, coupled with an equally clear future-vision, they are better able to manage change. It is these two components that provide direction, allowing companies to make better decisions as to "what to keep" and "what to change."

Vision statements answer the following questions – how would you answer them?

Who are we?

What is important to us?

What do we want to do?

What do want to become?

Viva La Difference

A company's vision is the foundation upon which competitive advantage is built. A sound core ideology along with an inspiring envisioned future not only gives direction when deciding what to keep and what to change, vision also provides a description upon which to identify what makes a company unique and different from their competitors.

Differentiating ourselves from the competition, as well as efforts to communicate what makes us unique, is only valuable when that uniqueness is of value to the customer. Customers don't care if what makes us unique is our product or service is blue when the competition's product is red unless they want blue products.

So the first step in communicating what makes your company different from the competition is aligning those differences with what you customers want – and the simplest way to do this is to ask them.

Asking customers what they want will give you the particulars related to your company's specific function or products. However, in general, what customers want can be stated in one word: **Velocity**. This is the speed at which you can get things moving and make things happen for your customer. No matter what your company's vision, the speed at which you can meet your customer's needs or solve their problems, as well as the ease your customer is able to get those needs met and problems solved is what differentiates your company from the competition.

While velocity is the primary competitive advantage, it can take many forms. Some potential differentiators include:

- PEOPLE
- RELATIONSHIPS
- Strategic Partnering
- Business FIT
- Design Innovation
- Technical Innovation
- Energy Efficiency
- Environmental Compliance
- Safety
- Total Cost of Construction
- Niche Expertise
- Project "Ownership"
- Client Experience

What are the specific means your company increases velocity for your customers? How does your company meet the customer's needs or solve their problems with greater velocity than your competition?

It Isn't About What – It's About Who

"Give me a long enough lever and a place to stand and I can lift the world" – Archimedes

In simple terms a lever is a tool that amplifies force - and when we leverage competitive advantages we amplify our efforts to win (and keep) business. The ancient scholar Archimedes was convinced he could actually move the world using a lever - if he only had a place to stand.

Picturing Archimedes moving the world with a lever we might identify the lever as his competitive advantage over some guy next to him trying to push the planet a little to the right using only brute force. But you'd be wrong. Archimedes is his own greatest competitive advantage. Without good old Archy who'd operate the lever?

This is a somewhat obvious way to introduce the fact that YOU are your company's greatest competitive advantage - but only when you follow the rules. This means you've got to be able to quantify your efforts, be able to provide proof of your value, and do things in your own, not easily duplicated, way.

Companies are comprised of individuals – and each and every "you" within that company represents that company's greatest competitive advantage. No matter "what" a company's competitive advantage, it is the people within the organization who make that advantage real to prospects and customers. The challenge is for companies to engage in principles and practices that leverage their people to their fullest potential.

Advantage Versus Average

We are not an average company, our service is not average, and we don't want our people to be average. We expect every employee to deliver WOW." - Tony Hsieh, Zappos

In 1999 Tony Hsieh, Alfred Lin, and Nick Swinmurn launched Zappos an online shoe store among thousands and thousands of online shoe stores, as well as hundreds of thousands of brick and mortar shoe stores.

- Their revenue at the end of that calendar year was 1.6 million.

- In 2001 their revenue was 8.6 million.

- By 2010 they'd hit one BILLION in revenue and made Fortune's Top 10.

So, what was their competitive advantage that grew a billion dollars?

People.

Zappos is the epitome of a company who understand only average companies compete on price or niche. Their competitive advantage? Creating a culture of WOW.

The Culture that Zappos Built

Zappos CEO Tony Hsieh is not your run-of-the-mill CEO, and his company is definitely not your run-of-the-mill company. In order to leave ordinary, he knew he had to build extraordinary, and he did that by using 5 principles designed to "Inspire, Engage, and WOW:

Principle #1: Develop Core Values – for real!

Principle #2: It's About the Customer

Principle #3: Business is Personal

Principle #4: Training is Essential

Principle #5: Reestablish Fun in the Workplace

Principle #1: Develop Core Values – for real!

Hsieh has shared that he actually resisted establishing any list of "core values" at Zappos, but their exponential growth led him to agree with another employee that doing so would provide some guidelines for hiring people who would be a good fit at Zappos.

But he wasn't in any rush. First off, he wasn't interested in core values that were more marketing messages than guiding principles. In a blog post Hsieh stated, "We wanted to make sure that didn't happen with our core values. We wanted a list of committable core values that we were willing to hire and fire on. If we weren't willing to do that, then they weren't really 'values'."

Second, Hsieh didn't take it upon himself to identify Zappos core values. Instead, over the course of years' time, he put out many emails to employees asking for their input. The fact that he did so demonstrates his deep understanding that people were Zappos greatest competitive advantage. He wanted to create corporate values that resonated and were able to truly drive employee behavior, not "end up being part of meaningless plaque on the wall of the corporate lobby."

And that's exactly what he got when, after a years' effort he and his fellow employees came up with Zappos 10 Core Values:

1. Deliver WOW Through Service

2. Embrace and Drive Change

3. Create Fun and A Little Weirdness

4. Be Adventurous, Creative, and Open-minded

5. Pursue Growth and Learning

6. Build Open and Honest Relationships With Communication

7. Build a Positive Team and Family Spirit

8. Do More With Less

9. Be Passionate and Determined

10. Be Humble

A couple questions you might want to ask yourself after reading Zappos Core Values:

When a new employee is brought on board are they immersed in your company's culture, or do you just preview coming attractions?

When you review your company's core values would be willing to use them as reasons to both "hire and fire"?

Principle #2: It's About the Customer

"... When a company masters ease and accuracy, its customers are looking for expedited service, knowledgeable staff, and other aspects of the service experience that add value." -Convergys

How many times have the words "we deliver the best customer service" come out of your mouth? Now ask yourself, "Do we really?" Because, if your answer is yes, this means that you are giving your customers what they want, when they want, and how they want.

Do you really *know* what your customers want?

You may already be ticking off a list in your head, but don't be surprised if that list is really just a list of features and benefits – not a list of what you customer *really* wants from you.

Remember, what customers want can be stated in one word: **Velocity** - the speed at which you can get things moving and make things happen for your customer.

What customers really want from you is a satisfactory and speedy solution to their service issue. What customers really want are people who bring them meaningful value. Customers *don't want* to "fight" or be the "squeaky wheel" in order to get their needs met or problems solved.

Now might good be a good time to ask yourself:

- Do you focus on the speed of your service?

- What is your reputation regarding service speed and effectiveness?

- Are your customers aware of your service velocity standards?

Principle #3: Business is Personal

"There is no better way for a brand…to put its money where its mouth (or heart) is than engaging in random acts of kindness."– Crucial Consumer Trends

Zappos gives us an incredibly moving story that demonstrates the power of making business a personal experience instead of a simple transaction.

A Zappos customer service agent once took a call from a woman who wanted to return a pair of shoes. Of course the best way to deter future returns is to discover the reason how or why the customer's needs weren't met or problems not solved. In this case the customer told the rep that her husband has just died and she didn't need the shoes anymore.

WOW.

Wow is right – and, because Zappos core value of "Delivering WOW Through Service" included training employees and empowering them to make independent decisions as to how to do that, the Zappo rep not only expressed her sincere condolences – when she got off the call she took the initiative to have flowers sent to the customer's home.

This random act of kindness on that reps' part then took on a life of its own when the customer shared her experience on Facebook. But getting hits on Facebook wasn't what motivated the rep to behave the way she did. What motivated her was being hired on the basis of her ability to demonstrate a commitment to the value of delivering WOW through customer service, and knowing her company would back up her decision as to how to do that.

This is a very powerful story – and brings up some questions we need to ask ourselves:

- What are the small and epic acts that make up your service story?

- How are you communicating the great stories of service that your company delivered?

Principle #4: Training is Essential

"Significant deficiencies exist among entrants at every educational level" or *"workforce readiness is one of the key issues facing the country."*–Workforce Readiness Report Cards

They say that Millennials (people born after 1982) are most likely going to be the best educated generation in history. However, as the above quote attests, level of education is not synonymous with workforce readiness. A majority of CEOs across industry sectors provide as one of their greatest challenges the fact that their pool of applicants does not represent a pool of applicants with skill sets that match their needs.

In other words, "education" does not train people with skills needed in the workplace.

This means it is up to the employer to provide that training. Sounds like a horrific threat to the welfare of business.

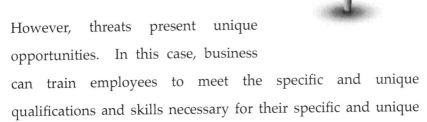

However, threats present unique opportunities. In this case, business can train employees to meet the specific and unique qualifications and skills necessary for their specific and unique business to create competitive advantage.

In the case of Zappos, all incoming employees attend a 4-week Customer Loyalty training course. At the end of this course (IF they pass – there are tales of C-suite level applicants not passing go) they are offered a significant cash incentive to quit. The fact that 97% refuse the incentive demonstrates the quality of training they receive.

Most of us would rather have multiple root canals than attend a four-week training course. But then maybe it is because we have never attended a training course delivered via the lens of a company whose culture is about the customer and who recognize their employees as their most competitive advantage.

And Zappos doesn't stop with this initial training. Every year they publish and annual "Culture Book" fostering not only a culture dedicated to the customer, but to continuous improvement as well.

Your experience with being trained, as well as providing training, might not measure up when compared to that of Zappos. If you're not convinced that it should be, knowing that 75% of Zappos billion dollar revenue is *repeat* business might lead you to ask yourself:

- What would happen if key employees left your business today?

- If you hire new employees straight out of college , etc., how workforce–ready are they?

- How am I preparing myself to be promoted and add greater value to my organization?

Principle #5: Reestablish Fun in the Workplace

"Innovation is the heart of the 'knowledge economy'–it is fundamentally social. The best ideas in any workplace arise out of casual contacts among different groups within the same company." – *Malcolm Gladwell*

Malcom Gladwell wrote a fantastic book called "The Tipping Point: How Little Things Can Make a Big Difference." One of those "little things" is "having fun." Even the most dreaded projects can be completed without drudgery when people have fun in the workplace.

At Zappos Tony Hsieh requires people to spend a certain amount of time "goofing off" with other employees from different departments throughout the company. Creativity is sparked when we have the opportunity to hear different perspectives regarding solving problems and meeting needs – and creativity is the mother of innovation.

Zappos employees also enjoy knowing that they are free to take a little siesta in the company "Nap Room" – knowing that "down time" is OK is a huge stress reducer and energizer, plus research has shown that a little daydreaming gets those creative juices flowing.

However, it is also up to the *employee* to infuse some fun at work. Zappos core values include being "adventurous" and "open-minded" – not to mention encouraging employees to create a little "weirdness." The "weird" is also "different" and different is often the road to "better."

Fun adds to feelings of excitement and when we are excited about what we are doing we are more productive.

This might be a good time to scratch our heads and wonder:

- What am I doing to enjoy my work more?

- What am I doing to help others enjoy their work more?

- What kind of fun things could my employer introduce in the workplace that would make me look forward to coming in?

- Who do I find to be the most "fun" people to work with? What is it that makes them fun?

Playing to Win

Zappos isn't Walmart – but that is exactly how they won their game. It would have been a completely different outcome if

Zappos had come onto the scene thinking the best advantage they had when it came to competing with Walmart, or any other competitor, was to do so on price. They would have lost the battle as well if they'd reverted to either of the two remaining choices The Big Three has to offer – quality or customer service. We already know The Big Three are simply the price of doing business.

Zappos become a Great company by not falling into the traps good companies set for themselves. Zappos followed The Rules and Zappos navigated their way past the common mistakes even good companies make when attempting to leverage their competitive advantages.

Zappos played to win – and you can too.

Planning to Win

Winning NFL coaches don't just run onto the field and expect to win every game because they know they've got some of the highest paid (price) and most talented (quality) team and offer their fans a stadium with the best seats and amenities (customer service). Doing that wouldn't even come close to leveraging the team's true competitive advantages. Counting on The Big Three doesn't give us a clue as to what our true competitive advantages are and, if you don't know what your competitive advantages are, you certainly can't develop strategies for winning that leverage competitive advantage.

Any strategy for winning must be based on true competitive advantage. You might have a lucky win – or even a lucky stretch – but luck certainly isn't a <u>sustainable </u>advantage.

If you want to win you've got to first identify existing, or create new, competitive advantages that follow The Rules (quantifiable, provable, not easily duplicated) and the only way to do *that* is to include a systematic appraisal of competitive advantages within your company's strategic planning session. Just make sure you don't jump from the frying pan into the fire during the process. It is important to remember that one of the most common mistakes even good companies make is thinking a strength is, by definition, a competitive advantage.

The Strong Survive – But Don't Always Win

A strength is not always a competitive advantage.

Certainly a company's strengths contribute to their success. However, when sweating out the old SWOT grid, the ability to place a number of strong suits in the strengths quadrant can create a false sense of security. Unfortunately, not all strengths are competitive advantages.

This seems a bit counter intuitive. How can a strength be anything *but* a competitive advantage? Answer: when it is just a strength.

If you've made this mistake in the past you might feel somewhat vindicated knowing even major world powers sometimes mistake strength as a competitive advantage. Take the case of Russia's TU Bear versus the United States' B2 Stealth.

In 1952 the Russians introduced the TU Bear (even the name sounds strong) as the major player in their strategic bomber arsenal. The craft was put into service in 1956 and is expected to continue to serve until at least 2040. Here are the TU Bear's pretty impressive strengths:

- Massive four-engine turboprop powered strategic bomb and missile platform
- World's fastest propeller-driven aircraft
- Propeller blades rotate faster than the speed of sound - known as "World's Noisiest Military Aircraft"
- Range of 7,800 miles

In 1999 the United States conducted the first public flight of the B2 or "Stealth" (has a strong ring to it) bomber. Like Russia's TU Bear, the Stealth bomber is a major player in America's strategic bomber arsenal. Here are the Stealth's imposing strengths:

- Capable of all-altitude attack missions
- Capable of penetrating extremely sophisticated air defense shields
- Can be deployed to anywhere in the world in a matter of hours
- Acoustic, infrared, visual and radar signatures make it difficult or impossible for opposition defenses to either detect, track or engage the B2

Both aircraft have definitive strengths, but you don't need to be a military strategist to determine not being easily detected is a definite competitive advantage for bomber or missile platform aircraft when what the competition offers is propeller blades rotating faster than sound resulting in the world's noisiest aircraft.

The Proof is in the Pudding

A competitive advantage can be proved.

Your average sales person may dream of a wardrobe that includes $150 shirts for every day of the week. Or maybe your closet already boasts expensive couture – either way, if you're going to purchase a shirt with a high price tag and touts their advantage to be quality - you're going to expect a product that can back this up.

As a matter-of-fact – and especially in today's economy – you might think any shirt company with such a high prices might want to lower their prices if they expect to survive.

Ike Behar clothiers knows better than that. Launched by Cuban immigrant Ike Behar in the 1960's this family owned company understands that price is *never* a competitive advantage.

Here is the competitive advantage that took Ike from fifty bucks in his pocket to the Fortune 500:

"We are great craftsman"…but can he prove it?

The importance of being able to back up a competitive advantage cannot be emphasized enough. This is where the "quality" pedal meets the metal. When Behar decided to sell his high-end shirts on the basis of quality he joined a plethora of other clothiers making the same claim.

Except he could prove it:

- Patented diamond quilted collars - No shrinking
- Single Needle Stitching-more durable
- Tight Stitching-18-22 stitches per inch; durability; look
- Handkerchief Rolled Seams-durability and crisp look

- Mother of Pearl Buttons-unbreakable; durable
- High Count Fabric-soft; durable; long lasting, crisp look
- 52 Total Steps-replicable process; consistency; quality
- Absolute Guarantee-100% no questions asked guarantee

When performing a systematic appraisal of your company's competitive advantages a simple way to discern whether or not they are "true" is whether or not you can provide proof that justifies the validity of your claim.

A Tough Act to Follow

A competitive advantage cannot be easily duplicated.

In today's franchised world the notion being unable to easily duplicate something identified as an advantage is actually NOT a competitive advantage seems, well, a bit antiquated.

Nothing could be further from the truth. How many startups have tried to duplicate a competitive advantage of the likes of a McDonalds or Taco Bell and lived to tell the tale? Actually, the opposite is true. Companies who've successfully taken the franchise mammoths on were those able to effectively differentiate themselves from these franchise giants.

Yet there is another, perhaps even more important, reason to consider something an advantage only when it cannot be easily replicated: sustainability.

As we all fondly remember, prior to 2009 our nation's economy supported what can only be described as a booming building industry. Business opportunities abounded like low growing fruit on an ever and fast-growing profit margin tree. Contractors could pick and choose from clients eager to get their show on the road who were more concerned about constructing their dream than what their dream was going to cost.

And then, as the saying goes, the bubble burst. But there are construction companies who continue to not only weather the storm, but thrive in an economic climate where opportunities no longer are a dime a dozen and once again contractors must artfully compete for business. In this new land of limited opportunities and budget-minded clients only companies with strong competitive advantages rule the day.

One such company is Flintco, a 90-year-old construction company dedicated to the continuous improvement necessary to win, and keep, a strong book of business even in these challenging times – and in ways that cannot be easily duplicated. Ways that Flincto enumerates in what they call "Zero by Design."

"ZERO By Design® is an integrated method of delivery, based on the best project management practices we have developed over a century in business. From partnering and preconstruction, to scheduling and safety, and even after the project is completed, ZERO By Design® covers project planning, safety, quality, scheduling and optimum client service standard procedures."

You might read that and think any construction company can say the same thing – they might be able to say it, but they'd have a hard time duplicating it because Flintco's Zero Design includes competitive advantages the competition finds (very) difficult to replicate:

- **Delivering on the Promise with ZERO By Design®** Flintco trains every employee in order to fully integrate all aspects of Zero by Design into every facet of their operations.

- **VALUE By Design™** Flintco has a complete "upfront preconstruction planning process that builds the project on paper before the first shovelful of dirt is turned." Most important, they are able to provide evidence of that value proving cost, time, and quality are enhanced.

- **Mission ZERO Partnering Meetings** Throughout every project Flintco regularly meets with owner, designers, and builders, sharing expertise and creating solutions. Their foundation for project success is collaborative cooperation.

- **ZERO Delays** Flintco is committed to zero delays by proactive scheduling management.

- **ZERO Punch List** This is definitely a tough act to follow, never mind duplicate. For anyone unfamiliar with the construction business, the "punch list" is a list of "completed" projects shown to be either missing, require finessing, or need replacement.

- **Eight ZERO Zero** Flintco gives their clients a toll-free number providing 24/7 service to their clients – even after their projects are complete. Most consider not being able to get their contractor on the phone the norm.

- **ZERO Accidents®** Accidents obviously have a negative impact on the employee and their family's welfare. They also add costs and delays for the consumer. Fintco has developed – and continuously implements – an award winning safety program.

By now you should be pretty familiar with the premise that a company's vision drives competitive advantage; to be competitive an advantage must follow The Rules; as well as to know what common mistakes to avoid when leveraging competitive advantage.   With all that under your belt you're ready to answer some very revealing questions:

- What do our customers want?
- What do we do that is unique?
- What are we known for?
- What do we do better than everyone else?
- How can we uniquely deliver our service?
- Do we have a unique competency?
- What factors drive our profitability?
- Do we compete in the right places?
- Are we strategically differentiated from our competitors?
- What specific problems do our customers experience that we might help them avoid?
- What are the strong and weak positions in our current product portfolio?

- What is the larger value chain of which we are a part, and is the overall   value chain capable of delivering maximum value to our customers?
- What continues to change externally---does it produce risk or opportunity?

Walmart Wins – Sometimes

Going up against Goliath was probably a rather intimidating experience for poor little David. Similarly, it is can seem rather intimidating attempting to leverage competitive advantage in the Walmart world we live in.

But appearances can be deceiving.

David would certainly have lost the battle had he tried to compete with Goliath on size. But he was smarter than that. Knowing he couldn't compete on size, he chose instead to leverage innovative technology - otherwise known as his trusty slingshot.

Every company has a trusty slingshot and, if they'll just take time to look and do the work, tons of stones to pick from to slay their particular Goliaths. From what you know now, discounting isn't one of those stones. Instead, take stock of your company using its vision as your guide to identify or create competitive advantages that increase the velocity of your customer's ability to get their needs met and/or solve their problems. These are the *only* advantages you can actually leverage. You may not be able to beat the competition on price, but you can follow the lead of these companies who successfully aimed their slingshots at Walmart – and won:

- **Walgreens:** Convenient locations, increased brand selection, smaller stores
- **Target:** Designer products, current trends, upscale (yet affordable) products
- **Best Buy:** Better quality products, larger selection, tech support
- **Costco:** higher end products (Dom Perigean, Cartier)
- **Pet Smart:** Greater variety, more products
- **Dicks Sporting Goods:** Larger variety of products, expert advice and training

Every one of these companies sells products similar to those on Walmart's shelves. Yet, each one of these companies differentiates themselves in ways that increase the velocity and ease in which a customer is able to get their needs met or problems solved. These advantages increase the velocity customers are able to get their needs met and problems solved – even when the customer compares these advantages to Walmart's price advantage. Not one of these competitors took

Walmart on using price discounting as a competitive advantage, yet each one of these companies successfully competes with Walmart.

Stop chasing your tail at best (or at worst drive your business into the ground) thinking price can be leveraged as a means to beat your competition. Instead, identify advantages that move your vision forward, follow The Rules, avoid common mistakes, and (most important) give your customers what they really want.

Post Chapter Exercise: Analyze Your Potential Advantages

Define the key product features that drive customer value. Potentially, there is a competitive advantage waiting to be discovered.

Value Drivers:	Definitions:
Service	The process of selecting, purchasing, and maintaining the product
Warranty	Warranty covers product or service for x years
Delivery	Delivery is free
Payment Options	Flexible payment terms are available

Functionality	Product or service meets or exceeds customer/consumer requirements
Support	Telephone & online support is available 24/7/365
Quality	Product or service has a reputation for being a leader in its category
Reliability	Product or service is available for use 24/7/365
Ease of Use	Product or service is easy to use and requires minimal instruction

Discover advantages that are quantifiable, provable, not easily duplicated, and relevant to your customer.

…ı depend on two rather unpredictable opportunities: luck and chance.

I know, there are those of you out there ready and able to point to a number of times games were won due to luck or chance – but, without that playbook, without a plan, the players most likely wouldn't have been able to identify the opportunity before it was lost.

No matter what your game, everybody wants to win, that's a given. But the people who win the most, people who become champions, don't just want to win, they plan to win.

This is especially true for professional sales people.

Sports metaphors abound when it comes to the subject of maximizing potential. For some, they might seem a bit cliché. If you happen to be leaning towards the "not another sports metaphor" side of the stadium, let me ask you this:

Do you view the desire to become a top performer in your chosen field as a sales professional to be too cliché to pursue?

I thought not.

There is a reason why sports metaphors are so apropos to those of us who have the honor to serve out our careers as professional sales persons – the desire to win resonates. We don't "close" sales – we win customers and clients. When something is "closed" it most often means the end of something. When we close a door we're usually finished with whatever we were doing on the other side of that door.

On the other hand, "winning" a client is akin to that football team winning their last game. Yes, it felt really great to win, but I guarantee you that every coach or player worth their salt takes away more than "a win." Running off that field they're already thinking about what they learned in the course of winning that particular game because they plan to keep winning.

Keyword: Plan.

Don't Drop the Ball

"I deeply believed that the teacher and coach who has the ability to properly plan...from both the daily and the long-range point of view together with the ability to devise the necessary drills to meet his particular needs for maximum efficiency, has tremendously increased his possibility of success."-Coach John Wooden

Many business and sales professionals will recognize the previous quote – but not because they're a fanatic fan of basketball.   True, Coach John Wooden brought his team to ten NCAA championships in twelve years and is also known for his 88 consecutive wins – but when people asked the man exactly what contributed most to his phenomenal success, he'd often answer with one his favorite sayings:

Failing to prepare is preparing to fail.

Stay Sharp

When we are properly prepared it means we have properly planned – and the first thing to prepare is your plan. One of Wooden's favorite historical mentors was Abraham Lincoln who, as we all know, was responsible for perhaps the biggest win our country has ever known: The Civil War. The man who won the war that saved our country liked to say if he had eight hours to chop down a tree he'd spend six of them sharpening his ax.

The point is that both Wooden and Lincoln understood that preparation was about taking care of the smallest details. They knew the smallest of details are what leads to great success.

Take that ax Lincoln spoke about. His choice of tool to make his point goes well beyond the obvious. Of course a sharp ax works better than a dull one. But, just for a moment, consider the monumental task that little ax performs. That tiny implement is responsible for taking down the entire tree.

Now let's take into consideration what Lincoln cited as the most important part of cutting that tree down successfully. Spending six hours devoted to sharpening an ax requires some good old fashioned discipline. Taking six hours to ensure a sharp edge to that blade definitely wasn't the exciting part. Certainly not as exciting as watching that tree hit the ground.

Iron Out Those Wrinkles

Like Lincoln, Wooden was pretty creative when it came to demonstrating to his players just how important little details were to winning a game. A famous story tells us of the first day of practice at UCLA. Surely all those players were eager to benefit from being coached by a legend. Can you imagine how they must have felt when Wooden spent 30 minutes instructing them how to put on their socks and lace up their shoes? Why was Wooden wasting their time on such an insignificant detail?

Of course, as usual, Wooden nimbly made his point: if the players had wrinkles in their socks or their shoes weren't tied correctly they'd leave themselves open to getting blisters. Blisters meant missing practice. Missing practice meant they could not hit the court come game time.

Not playing meant not winning.

Wooden told them "If you want to win championships, you must take care of the smallest of details."

Putting on socks correctly as well as tying laces appropriately were both, all be they small, processes necessary in order to win.

The Three P's: Passion, Process, and Plan

Similarly, knowing we've got deadlines to hit and goals to meet (sometimes within seemingly impossible time frames) it is easy to fall into the trap of thinking taking time to "plan" just how to meet those deadlines and goals is a waste of time that could be better spent working in the field. After all you're totally fired up and passionate about meeting your goals. You're revved up and motivated to run right out into the field and win the game.

The problem is, unless we develop the discipline to take the time to plan all those little details that add up to big success (processes), we all too often find ourselves out on that field with little idea as to how to proceed.

While passion is definitely the fuel that fires our motivation to succeed, unless we have disciplined ourselves to first create (and then follow) a plan, that motivation all too quickly dries up when we fail to perform at the level necessary to meet our deadlines and achieve our goals. In a nutshell, in order to achieve we must perform.

Our passion motivates, but it is our plan that drives performance.

Planning is the means to install the discipline necessary to ensure that we've considered every detail, no matter how small, that contributes to our success – whether we define that success as winning a specific customer, or achieving our overall goals.

Become a Natural

For those of you who just don't happen to be into football or basketball, let's use another sports-related metaphor that might better resonate – the Olympics. In particular, figure skating. The best figure skaters are so exceptional at what they do they make it look easy. Of course we know they've trained for years but, the second that blade hits the ice, movement just flows as if defying the laws of physics on ice was the most natural thing in the world to do.

Most sales professionals have had similar experiences watching those we may consider to be "naturals" at work; we might even be a bit jealous. Maybe even excused our own less-than-top performance by thinking if things came that "easy" to us we'd be twice as successful when you consider all the work we put into it, whereas it looks like that "Top 5%" person effortlessly places decision-makers makers under some kind of trance where they pull out their pens ready to sign.

Looks can be deceiving.

No matter how "easy" or "natural" it may appear to be for someone else who is consistently performing at a level you covet, but have not yet been able to achieve – you can be guaranteed that person has a plan and follows it consistently and meticulously.

Planning is natural to succeeding.

Consider the Customer

Things have definitely changed for sales professionals. No longer can we rely on "tried and true" notions of closing (winning) sales by rattling off the superiority of our company and product in the market; how superior the features and benefits of our products and services; or how doing business with us represents adding significant value to their purchase.

But one thing hasn't changed and that's the fact that the customer is (still) always right. As a matter-of-fact, today your customer is more right than they've ever been because they are more informed.   Technology has created a "more evolved" customer.

Don't Confuse Process with Planning

Because we're now dealing with customers who know what they want – the key to success becomes planning our process.

It is because customers have become more savvy that many companies as well as individual sales professionals have instituted formal sales processes. However, there are countless companies and professionals baffled as to why their processes have not maximized revenue as anticipated.

Of course there may be gaps in their process (this is quite common) that could be cited as the missing link for success, but, even more often, the greatest contributor for sales processes failing to reap what they sow is a failure to plan; failure to follow the plan; and/or failure to consistently assess the plan and modify the plan when necessary.

However, unfortunately perhaps the most common factor contributing to sales processes failing is confusing the function of "process" with the function of "plan."

A process is a series of actions that can be taught, duplicated, and repeated over and over with consistent results. Businesses are built by following processes - accounting processes, procurement processes, human resources processes – and, of course, business development processes. Each of these processes is designed for the express purpose of creating value. In the case of business development it goes without saying that value is identified as the ability of any sales process we design and follow to contribute to winning sales.

On the other hand, a plan is a written document that describes specific courses of action (processes) designed to achieve specific goals and then assigns a specific order as well as specific timeframes for each process to be completed.

If you're still not clear on the difference between process and plan, let's take a little trip to help clarify the difference.

We've all looked forward to taking a long awaited vacation. For the purposes of this example we'll say that you've decided the family would enjoy a trip to Disneyworld and certainly getting the family to Disneyworld is a process. There is a process of putting in for the time off with your employer; a process of putting aside the necessary funds; the process of procuring the most cost-effective means of travel and lodging; a process of packing the necessary clothing and equipment; the process of examining family member's schedules to identify any conflicts; not to mention the process of discovering the wants and desires of individual family members during the trip.

All of the processes associated with taking that vacation require planning.

For instance, your employer may require you make the request for time off within a specific time frame. Your spouse needs to arrange their own time off. You need to review your budget to discover how much you can save and how long it is going to take to save funds needed for the trip. You have to research and compare modes of travel as well as lodging choices.

If you don't have a plan that not only describes the various activities that need to take place before you take off on that trip, but also the order and timeframes they need to take place in – what you wanted to be a relaxing vacation can easily turn into a nightmare.

This little vignette also demonstrates the most powerful thing about having and following a plan: the ability to identify when your processes aren't producing value.

In our Disneyland example, you decided that the family would like a nice trip to Disney World. Because you created and then followed a plan to complete all of the necessary processes in a specific and logical order within specific timeframes, you are surprised to discover your family doesn't want to go to Disney World at all – they want to go camping.

You were correct in thinking the family wanted to go on a vacation, you knew they'd really enjoyed going to Disneyland in the past – but you misidentified what they wanted this vacation to be. And you discovered that before you put down any of those pesky nonrefundable deposits.

The point of the story is that sales professionals often find themselves in similar situations where they've decided what their customers want and then follow processes designed to sell them what they've decided their customer wants. The decision that sales person made to try to sell their customer what they think the customer wanted was probably based on past experience with that customer.

It is only when you have both sales processes designed to create value as well as a plan to implement these processes within a logical order and specific timeframes that you have put yourself in a position where you don't waste resources (i.e. your time and effort) attempting to sell something to customers they either don't want, don't need anymore, or aren't ready for.

PART II

Sales Process Plus++™

..For The Professional Office

"Selling is a Contact Sport"

Sales Process Plus™

"The companies greatest competitive advantage is a disciplined process driven sales professional.."

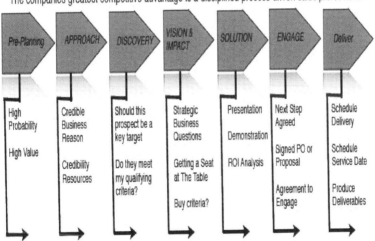

Pre-Planning	APPROACH	DISCOVERY	VISION & IMPACT	SOLUTION	ENGAGE	Deliver
High Probability	Credible Business Reason	Should this prospect be a key target	Strategic Business Questions	Presentation	Next Step Agreed	Schedule Delivery
High Value	Credibility Resources	Do they meet my qualifying criteria?	Getting a Seat at The Table	Demonstration	Signed PO or Proposal	Schedule Service Date
			Buy criteria?	ROI Analysis	Agreement to Engage	Produce Deliverables

SALES PROCESS

What is Process?

"The sole function of business is to develop a customer"--Peter
Drucker

Process improvement has swept the country.   Companies are
working hard to dramatically improve quality, service,
productivity, and profitability. If you want something done right
and you want it done consistently right, then you create a
disciplined, well-defined process to produce the results desired.

> A "process" is a series of step-by-step guidelines that are designed to:
>
> 1) Create consistent performance,
>
> 2) Allow for measurement of critical areas, and
>
> 3) To provide the ability to troubleshoot variance or failure.

Without a process, a series of actions that can be taught,
measured, and duplicated over and over, consistent results will be elusive at
best and nonexistent at worst. There has literally been millions of

dollars spent on Total Quality Management during the quality revolution of the 1980's. Unfortunately, the marketing and sales functions did not get the attention that other parts of the corporation enjoyed.

Organizations are a collection of processes. These processes are the natural business activities that typically produce value, serve customers, and generate income for the business. Organizations that best manage these processes can develop advantages that lead to greater success. In fact, an organization's greatest competitive advantage is a disciplined, process-oriented sales professional.

The first step in a sales process is to map the process from lead generation to a prospect becoming a long-term customer. Using a process map is a good first step. The process map should consist of a visual diagram of

> "If you can't describe what you are doing as a process, you don't know what you are doing"- W. Edwards Deming

the process and the tools that enable you to document, analyze, improve, and manage the process.

A sales organization that understands the interrelationship of each step in the process can develop consistency, the ability to replicate, and accountability. Here are a few other benefits of using a process map to consider:

•Identification of process flaws that create consistent problems and reduce the company's closing ratio;

•The opportunity to identify the activities that add value to the customer and improve closing ratios;

•Improvement of efficiencies and customer satisfaction; and

•Identification of areas that are "churning" the company's resources unnecessarily.

The Demise of the Sales Profession?

Several years ago, Walmart initiated a study to determine if the 3,800 buying agents employed were efficient and warranted the expense on the company's bottom line. It was a wake-up call for the sales profession. Walmart was determined to streamline their buying process and determined that salespeople did not add value and were no longer welcome. Walmart took the stance that if we need something, we will call you.

Unfortunately, Walmart in general was correct. Why should they listen to a salesperson to save a few pennies? Couldn't they achieve the same results by researching product on the internet?

In Marc Miller's book <u>A Seat At The Table</u>, (Miller2010) he argues that customers today are looking for value in the form of help--specifically, strategic help. The days of canned pitches or simply pushing product are over. Unfortunately, it is difficult to convince some individuals and organizations of this fact.

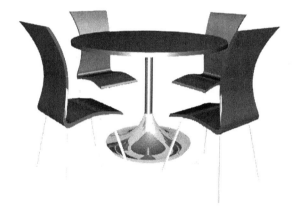

Essentially, sales has a new role to play and it involves two main parts. First, help satisfy the urgent short-term need. Second, devise solutions that will help the customer achieve or expand their master strategies. This takes a disciplined, process-oriented sales professional.

So "the demise of the sales profession" is a false statement, but we do need to make some changes. Have you ever noticed that about 5% of a company's sales team significantly achieves greater results than the remaining 95%? Why?

Symptoms of Process Deficiencies

There have been a significant number of businesses that failed during our economic downturn. On the other hand, there have been many small businesses that are thriving. Why? What is going on? How does the sales process relate?

Sales process allows us to examine where business development breaks down. Many of us are trying to persuade our small-business clients to look at marketing and sales as a "production system." In the manufacturing process, each step can be analyzed and improved. Project management follows a strict set of process guidelines. Accounting uses a well-defined process to create consistent outcomes. In most any department inside almost any company you will find a process, or a series of processes, that is used to create accuracy, consistency, and dependability. The marketing and sales department can and should be managed in the same way. If a sales process will help create consistent results, while providing the ability to determine a specific cause of sales failure, why do the majority of companies not have one?

There are several symptoms within the sales process that can be identified and indicate there may be a sales-process breakdown. Many of these "breakdowns" directly impact the Sales Revenue Model.

The Sales Revenue Model

Gross Margin Revenues = (Opportunities x Win Percentage) x (Opportunity Value x Margin Percentage) x Frequency.

Breakdowns having an impact on the Sales Revenue Model include:

- Business cycle is too long. This affects the model by delaying new orders and reducing revenue during the company's business cycle.

- Profit margins are too low, thus reducing the gross profit to the company.

- Sales have become stagnant due to a poor pipeline. A sales process will define specifically how the salesperson and the organization develop prospects. It directly affects the "opportunity" element of the Sales Revenue model.

- Salespeople report chaos in the sales cycle or sales call, primarily due to not understanding how to move an opportunity forward. This has an impact on the Win Percentage element.

- Too many costly errors being made and company resources being unnecessarily churned. Typically, this is due to shortcutting or altogether skipping the qualifying step. This has an impact on the Win Percentage element.

- Company is producing adequate leads but not converting to customers. Again, customers have become more complex. Customers are looking for sales professionals who can solve their short-term urgent needs and engage as a partner to solve long-term strategic needs.

- Products are being returned at a greater rate than the industry average due to not understanding the customer's true needs. This has a direct impact on the Margin Percentage element of the Sales Revenue model.

- New salesperson ramp-up time is 2-3 times longer than planned. How do you on-board a new salesperson without a process to train to?

- Salespeople cannot communicate what makes them successful because they cannot point to the process. In all likelihood, the salesperson is not reaching their true potential even though they are having some success.

- Poor forecasting is the norm. Sales process helps you quantify and predict sales on a consistent, replicable basis.

- Market trending is not detected until the damage is done and the competitor has developed an advantage.

- New product launches fail or get poor results.

- Salespeople talk too much and are less effective because they feel chaos when they do not understand what to do next.

- Productive selling time is too low and impacts all elements of the Sales Revenue model.

Predictable Challenges

Without a defined sales process, companies will face predictable challenges. To summarize some of the key points:

When a salesperson is successful, you will not know exactly why. Is she a great salesperson, or just lucky? Why exactly did she win that particular sale? Can she do it again?

When a salesperson is unsuccessful, you will not know exactly why. Was the price too high or the product poorly differentiated? Did he make a bad presentation, or was it an unqualified prospect? Did he lose to a competitor, or simply fail to ask for the order?

It will be hard to determine how to train new salespeople because you are not sure which skills contribute most, or least, to success. Thus, companies focus on product training and exclude selling-skills training.

It is extremely difficult for the company to help a struggling salesperson improve because you are not sure which skills contribute most, or least, to success.

Unable to produce consistent results, or clearly identify

performance barriers, companies tend to cling to the theory that they must hire the "born salesperson."

Without a well-defined and documented sales process, the sales manager's job is considerably more difficult. Some sales professionals may be incredibly talented but need to be educated on the sales process to develop consistency. Some salespeople may need skills development. It is frustrating when sales become

> *"The hit and miss pitch techniques that were the mainstay of selling in calmer years can't even begin to address--sales in today's super heated markets"* -- Robert B. Miller

stagnant and the manager does not know how to correct. Typically, sales is told to just work harder, make more calls, or try to ask better questions. Who knows?

Sales process is a production system that will produce more consistent results. What affect would it have on your business if you could significantly increase your Win Percentage? A defined sales process (in combination with a good understanding of the sales metrics) creates more opportunities, higher opportunity values, more qualified opportunities, and far more effective sales presentations that will gain you a "seat at the table."

Ultimately, salespeople should find themselves presenting the right solution, one that takes both short-term urgent and long-term business strategies into account.

"For us, it's all about helping the client achieve their objectives first. That's the order--client first, us second, I believe this mind set--along with sales process--truly differentiates our company"-Paul Schleuter, Executive Vice President, Global Sales, Oerlikon/Fairfield

How to Implement a Sales Process:

- Engage a Sales Process Engineer who can assist you in mapping a custom sales process;

- Document the steps to a successful sales transaction from a lead to a customer making multiple purchases;

- Design the process after step analysis and mapping;

- Train your sales team and educate them on the benefits of a well-designed process; and

- Support and implement accountability measures.

There Is No Time to Waste

There is no perfect time to implement a sales process. Your sales and marketing teams will have to engage. One thing is sure-- after completing the development, your customers will see greater value from your teams and start to see you more as a strategic resource rather than a company pushing products. Just going through the process and getting marketing and sales thinking like a production unit will produce positive results. David Maister, author of The Trusted Advisor and True Professionalism, (Maister, 1997) is one of the chief proponents of consultive-type selling in which a company adds value by truly understanding customer's needs. A sales process forces a sale representative to become consultative in theory. (However, the salesperson may lack the skills to perform at the high level of a consultative salesperson.)

Finally, be aware that the Walmart scare woke up the industry. Your competitors may bring "sales process" selling to your customer before you do. Michael J. Webb, author of Sales and Marketing the Six Sigma Way (Webb, 2006) is one of the leading authorities on sales process, calls this the "first-mover advantage." To be the second mover on something this innovative may permanently relegate your company to second tier status."

Sales Process PLUS++

...for the Professional Office™ (advise)

PROCESS	STEP
Approach	1
Discovery	2
Vision & **I**mplication	3
Solution	4
Engage	5

APPROACH

It's ironic, but what most sales professionals dread the most is being treated like a salesperson. This isn't true in most professions. Being identified as a doctor doesn't cause a physician undue anxiety. Firefighters usually get a thumbs up. And people usually don't avoid taking a call from their accountant.

Step # 1

Approach

Discovery

Vision & Implication

Solution

Engagement

You might think attorneys share a similar trepidation, but judging from the plethora of television ads, it's obvious attorneys not only don't dread, but actively encourage, people to treat them like a lawyer.

But being tagged as that "Sales Guy" (or Gal) is different. The question is why and the answer is rather obvious. People view those other professionals as doing something for them or bringing something to them that meets their needs or solves their problems; whereas people have a tendency to treat sales professionals as "That Sales Guy" because they perceive the sales person wants something from them.

And they are essentially correct. After all, you do want to win the sale.

If you're a professional who dreads being treated like a salesperson, the first step is to take a deep breath and honestly examine your sales approach to ensure you're not behaving like one.

Traditional Sales Approaches

Traditions can be a very powerful means to maintain valuable status quos. For example, retailers traditionally hold sales during holidays. Customers value this tradition and via this tradition the retailer maintains a status quo of increased sales during specific periods.

Retail businesses maintain this tradition for one simple reason: it works.

Traditions can buoy business when they work, but maintaining traditions that no longer work act as anchors that drag us down – and this is especially true for today's sales professional. Let's take a walk down (what should be) memory lane and review three traditional "That Sales Guy" approaches.

Tradition #1: The Canned Sales Presentation

It is common knowledge within the sales profession that canned sales presentations are strictly structured and scripted presentations meant to be memorized and not deviated from. The focus of the scripted sales presentation is on features and benefits of the product.

This is an excellent first example because most sales professionals will dismiss it as an approach used only by telemarketers and in door-to-door sales. As a matter-of-fact you may even consider this approach an insult to the profession. Canning is for tuna fish, not professional sales. However, after a close and honest evaluation of your approach it isn't unusual to find uncomfortable remnants of this outdated and ineffective sales technique.

Tradition #2: Stimulus – Response Approach

Very similar to a canned approach, but relies on the salesperson presenting specific "stimuli" (usually features and/or benefits) in a particular sequence styled to elicit a specific response on the part of the customer. The ultimate response desired is, of course, the sale. However, the SR approach also dangles specific phrasing or types of questions like carrots to stimulate specific responses from the prospect in a sequential manner that ultimately closes the sale.

But customers aren't as easily trained as Pavlov's dogs.

You may think you threw this out of the tool box long ago, or perhaps have never even (at least consciously) used this approach. But you may be surprised when, after reviewing your usual approach, how often you use the same methods (stimuli) to get your desired result (response) simply because they have become habitual. Habits, like traditions, can be useful– but only when they work.

Tradition #3: Formula Selling

Formula selling is any type of approach centered on defined stages designed to lead the potential customer to make a purchase. While formula selling may differ in the number and categories of stages, the most familiar formula selling approach is AIDA: Attention, Interest, Desire, and Action.

Formula selling shares deficits with both canned and SR, but what is most notable about AIDA type approaches is the focus shifts from "training" (which most customers find synonymous with "tricking") a customer to buy, to leading the customer down an artificial garden path the ends with the sale.

All of these approaches had their day. But today's educated, savvy customers don't appreciate being canned, trained, or lead. Today's customer resents being manipulated and, if your customer smells even a whiff of these outdated approaches, you run the risk of being treated like a salesperson – except when it comes to winning the sale.

The Credibility Factor

The common factor that outdated, ineffective sales approaches share is that not one of them engenders the most important quality a sales professional needs to communicate to their customer:

"You can trust me."

Traditional sales approaches are just that: the way to approach a sale - not the way to approach a customer. We've already established how traditional approaches encourage your customer to perceive you as someone who wants something from them instead of someone who can do something for them.

Traditional sales approaches don't establish the credibility of the salesperson with their customer and, without that credibility, it is impossible for your customer to trust you. Credibility is the first step in the process of establishing yourself to be someone your customer can believe deserves their trust.

Take a sales person who has expert knowledge about their product. It would appear that this knowledge would be enough to inspire the customer to place their trust in that sales person.

However, expert knowledge in and of itself is a credential – all knowledge about product does is qualify that sales person as an expert. Knowledge alone does not qualify that salesperson as someone who is credible (believable) and who can be trusted. Credentials are only one component of credibility.

Enhancing Credibility

The successful sales professionals understand the Power of Process and Enhancing Credibility are second only to Planning in the sales process continuum. Process is a set of actions and actions are behaviors. This is an incredibly important concept for two reasons:

1.   Customer's don't assign credibility or base their ability to trust a sales professional solely on their credentials – rather they judge the credibility of those very credentials on that sales person's behavior, and;

2.   Sales professionals can enhance their credibility via specific, process-oriented behaviors.

Conveying Credibility

Conveying credibility is integral to the process of creating trust. Conveying credibility with your customer is how you earn the right to their trust.

We've discussed how credentials are an important element of credibility but, no matter how impressive those credentials are, if your behaviors don't back those credentials up; you will lose credibility with your customer.

Here are some very specific behaviors to enhance credibility with your customer:

- Don't lie.

- Don't exaggerate. At all. Ever.

- Be passionate.

- Use your references.

- If you don't know--say so.

- Communicate competitive advantage.

- Demonstrate a relaxed, friendly presence.

- Plan, do your homework.

While credentials alone don't create credibility, the main elements that establish credibility often have credentials associated with them. Take a look at the following elements of credibility. Ask yourself:

What personal qualities or credentials do I possess within each of these categories?

What process and/or behaviors do I engage in that back up my credentials?

- Experience

- Knowledge

- Presentation

- Associations

Detecting Your Customer Credibility Factor

We'd all like to think we behave in ways that enhance our credibility with customers. You might even have just skimmed through this section thinking your customers find you inordinately credible and none of this pertains to you. However, resting on our laurels isn't how we get ahead. Instead, consistent and continuous improvement is what drives our performance onward and upward.

Fortunately your "Customer Credibility Factor" can be pretty easily determined by not only examining your own process and behavior – but that of your customers as well.

It doesn't require an advanced degree to notice when you are losing credibility during a sales call. Just look out for the following indicators:

• You note general negative body language on the part of your customer.

• Your customer has their arms folded across their chest.

• Your customer is fidgeting (i.e. tapping their pen or foot).

• Your customer is leaning away from you. Worse yet, leaning away with their hands over their head.

• Your customer yawns periodically (this is a dead giveaway).

• Your customer allows, and may even seem to invite, outside interruptions.

• Your gut is churning (another dead giveaway, it is advisable to always listen to your gut).

• Your customer throws out issues centered on power/ control.

On the flip side, here are some definite signs that your Customer Credibility Factor is high:

- You note general positive body language on the part of your customer.

- Your customer nods in agreement with you as you are speaking.

- Your customer shares examples and/or stories with you

- Your customer is smiling, perhaps throws a few humorous quips into the conversation.

- Your customer doesn't allow interruptions (this is an extremely good sign.)

- Your customer voluntarily and eagerly participates in the conversation.

- Your customer wants to talk about solutions.

The Trusted Advisor

The best way to inspire people is to convince them by everything you do, and by your everyday attitude, that you are wholeheartedly supporting them.

Someone who behaves like a salesperson will always be "That Sales Guy" (or Gal).

The surprising truth is that the sales approach that works isn't a sales approach at all – rather the most successful approach is to approach your customer as their Trusted Advisor.

There is no higher calling for a sales professional than to become a Trusted Advisor to their customers. A Trusted Advisor develops a relationship that is focused on the customer's vision of the business. Customers who perceive you to be a Trusted Advisor believe that you are sincerely dedicated to serving their best interests and can be completely trusted to serve those interests via a long-relationship based on honesty and genuine personal rapport.

Benefits of the Trusted Advisor Role

The benefits of serving as a Trusted Advisor to your customers are vast. The professional sales person who stands as a primary resource for their customer's to rely on to assist solving their problems and provide support needed to achieve their goals is able to establish a level of deep credibility and trust with that client – a position that clearly puts that salesperson in a position to win sales within their offering related to solving the customers problems and achieving the customers goals.

When a Trusted Advisor extends the relationship with their customer to include the ability to provide that customer with trusted advice, information, and connections outside the borders of their product and/or service line, that salesperson also expands their potential customer base.

Reaching the status of Trusted Advisor doesn't happen overnight. Like any long-term relationship of value it is a relationship that requires work and is strengthened over time.

While it may be possible to worm one's way into a cheap imitation of a Trusted Advisor solely for the purpose of reaping the benefits of the role, because the customer places such high priorities on sincerity and honesty, that relationship will never fully flower and is certain to be short-term.

The Elements of Trust

Becoming a Trusted Advisor requires a deep understanding of the elements of trust. The Credibility Factor rendered credibility as a self-evident component of trust. However, just as credentials are only one component of credibility, in turn, credibility is only one component of trust.

Trust is actually a complex of very specific qualities:

• Expertise and Experience

• Dependability

• Rapport

• Level of Self-Orientation

Dependability

One foundation of trust is the ability, proven by experience, to be able to count on someone to be consistently dependable. A reliable sales professional:

- Delivers commitments on time.

- Provides agendas up front.

- Expresses goals clearly and transparently.

- Consistently meets or exceeds expectations.

- Respects the other's time by reconfirming scheduled events.

Although fictional, the movie <u>Castaway</u> starring Tom Hanks provides us with an excellent example of the power of reliability as well as its role in creating trust. Although marooned on an island for years, Hanks' character, a FedEx employee, makes sure a package found on the island sent in their care gets delivered after he returns.

FedEx has a reputation for reliably delivering packages correctly, undamaged, and on time. However, it doesn't stop there. FedEx consistently demonstrates their reliability throughout all company processes and messages.

- First ring response

- Smooth voicemail interface

- Knowledgeable, energetic associates

- Consistent packaging

- Consistent Zip Strip Example

- Consistent branding on vehicles

- Uniforms and professionalism

- Accurate tracking system

- Low driver turnover rate

- Consistent drop off locations

Sales professionals will do well who emulate the high level reliability demonstrated by FedEx.

In what ways do you consistently demonstrate reliability to your customers and prospects?

Rapport or Intimacy

Traditionally most of us have been counseled not to create personal relationships in the workplace. Rather relationships with colleagues and customers should be business oriented and impersonal in nature. However, intimacy within a relationship requires a level of transparency between the parties that promotes honesty and creates trust.

People want to do business with people they know, like, and trust. It is obvious a significant level of intimacy is required in order to get to know someone enough to like and trust them.

Level of Self-Orientation

Self-orientation can be defined as the degree to which a person is more interested in achieving their own personal agenda in a relationship than fostering a mutually beneficial relationship.

Trust is actually a sum that is greater than its parts, but it can be helpful to view it as an equation:

Trust = (Experience/Expertise + Dependability + Rapport) divided by Level of Self-Orientation

Nobody wants to think of themselves as self-serving or self-centered, both of which are telltale signs of high levels of self-orientation. Although spotting someone with a high level of self-orientation seems fairly obvious to us, it is more difficult to evaluate our own. Here are a few helpful questions you can ask yourself to assist you to see things about yourself that may be all too obvious to others:

•   Do I like to tell stories about myself that have no purpose other than making me the center of the conversation?

•   Do I have a habit of too quickly finishing someone

sentences?

- Do lulls in a conversation make me uncomfortable, so much so that I feel compelled to speak?

- Do I have a strong need to appear clever, bright, and/or witty?

- Do I habitually not answer questions directly?

- Am I unwilling to say I don't know?

- Do I drop names more to impress than assist?

- Do I have a tendency to want to have the last word?

- Do I tend to stop actively listening to my customers?

- Do I excessively share my qualifications or credentials?

High Impact Behavior for Building Trust

Knowing what not to do when it comes to building trust isn't enough. Engaging in high impact trust building behaviors, along with doing your homework as to how to provide meaningful assistance and contributions to our customer's success, show if you've got what it takes to become a Trusted Advisor.

Again, sales professional should ensure these high impact, trust building behaviors are built into their process.

- Listen to everything.

- Empathize (for real).

- Build a shared agenda of "give-get."

- Take a chance and go out on a limb.

- Ask great questions.

- Give good ideas away as added value.

- Return calls fast.

Remember demonstrating your trustworthiness as well as demonstrating the ability to deliver valuable advice and assistance takes time – don't rush it. Every single interaction with your customers is an opportunity to approach your customer and take another step closer to becoming their Trusted Advisor.

Although some specific elements of traditional sales approaches still stand, the approaches themselves fail over time because they are focused on winning the sale. Sales processes and behaviors dedicated to serving in the capacity of a Trusted Advisor is the only method that places the customer before your intent to win the sale. This approach takes time, but it is time spent creating long-term customer relationships. Although this focus and processes associated with it may be counterintuitive, not to mention a little scary when striving to meet and exceed your sales goals, Trusted Advisor sales professionals are top shelf income producers.

Post Chapter Exercise:

1. List 5 things that indicate you have developed credibility with your customer or client?

2. How can you enhance credibility?

3. Can you apply the trust formula to your day-to-day work?

4. Why is your "self-orientation" so critical to your approach and earning the right?

5. What are high impact activities that will increase your level of trust?

6. Create your credible business reason and "test."

7. Role-play the first 7 minutes of your sales presentation. Do you consistently achieve credibility?

DISCOVERY

This is an important chapter, so let's get right down to business. The most important resource a professional salesperson has is time, and time is a precious as well as limited resource – and there's no greater waste of time when it comes to maximizing revenue than spending it on an improperly or unqualified prospect.

Step # 2

Approach

Discovery

Vision & Implication

Solution

Engagement

It follows that the absolute best use of your time as a professional sales person is to spend it creating and implementing a prospect qualifying process specific to your industry sector.

Before we get into the meat of the matter, let's try a little mind experiment.

Picture a day in the last week or so that you feel was particularly busy. Start at the beginning and then move through as many tasks and activities you can remember in the order you completed them. Now, attach a dollar sign to that day.

You might feel pretty good about the number you've come up

with. Your day included a number of potential wins that could translate into very healthy income. But now ask yourself the following questions about each of those opportunities:

- Is it budgeted?

- What is the application?

- How much do they need?

- Who is the competition?

- Target price?

- When do they need it?

- Why would they buy from me? (Value proposition)

Now take a look at the following statistics:

- When you can answer all 7 questions 90% of orders are booked.

- When you can answer 4-6 of these questions booking rate drops to 10%.

- If you can answer 3 or less, you're looking at closing only 1%.

The above statistics come from twenty years of tracking the impact of a well-thought out, well-planned prospect qualifying process. Only when you can provide definitive answers to at least 4 of those questions should you consider a prospect as having been qualified.

Qualifying the Prospect is in Your Customer's Best Interest

Normally when we think of what it means to qualify a prospect we think only in terms of a method of making sure they meet specific criteria necessary in order to win the sale, which is a pretty natural assumption. It's pretty easy to assume that the primary purpose of asking (and getting the answer) to those very important seven questions is discovering whether or not the prospect meets the criteria necessary to purchase your specific offering. However, the most important information gleaned in the process of qualifying a prospect is whether or not pursuing the prospect is a good use of time.

Spending your time working with a prospect means investing in that prospect. Investing your time without investigating the return that can be expected from a prospect is just as irresponsible as investing money in the stock market just because they're listed on the exchange.

But it isn't only your time you need to be concerned about. You don't want to waste the prospect's time either. There's no greater way to alienate a prospect, or current account for that matter, than to waste their time. One thing that will always be true is that things change. A prospect that doesn't qualify today may qualify in the future. If you spent that prospect's time by jumping into a product presentation the first time you met, there's a good chance you wasted their time and a willingness to waste your customer's time isn't a competitive advantage. When the day comes that the prospect does qualify, having previously wasted their time isn't what's going to compel them to pick up the phone to call you back in.

On the other hand, when working with a prospect means taking time to qualify the prospect, you respect that prospect's time. When a prospect is qualified correctly, that process is of value to your potential future customer. For example, asking whether or not the purchase has been budgeted provides the opportunity for the prospect to more closely examine how well their budget positions them for growth. Discussing the competition provides the prospect with the opportunity to reevaluate their needs and can even uncover a problem they didn't know they had.

Most of all, properly qualifying a prospect is an opportunity to engender trust between yourself and your prospect. Qualifying conversations and communications give your prospect reason to believe that you are sincerely interested in serving their best interests. Remember that the Top 5% of sales professionals in the domestic United States build their book of business on trust.

It's the Principle of the Thing

If we get push back on spending time qualifying customers, it's usually some sort of counter to the idea that working unqualified prospects is a waste of time. After all, isn't sales is a numbers game? Doesn't that mean the more people you get in front of, the greater the opportunity to win? We've already established that qualifying a customer is a chance to win the trust of a prospect – so doesn't it make sense a good use of time is winning the trust of as many prospects as possible?

Most of you are probably well aware of the Pareto Principle, or the "80/20 Rule." What started out as an observation made by Italian economist Vilfredo Pareto that 20% of the country's population owned 80% of the country's accumulated wealth, has become a general rule of thumb when it comes to management. This evolution of Pareto's original observation is credited to Joseph M. Juran, a pioneer in quality management, who generalized Pareto's observation into a principle that states a small number of causes are responsible for a large percentage of total effect. In other words, the relationship between input and output isn't balanced.

In plain English, the Pareto Principle means that most of us put most of our time into efforts that don't deliver the intended results. In even plainer language, it means too many professional sales people are spinning their wheels wasting time on efforts that do little or nothing to maximize revenue.

The "80/20" ratio of the Pareto Principle is relative. You could just as easily say that 80% of input creates 10% of outcome. The usefulness of the principle doesn't lie in an exact ratio or an even understanding the unequal relationship between what we put into something and what we get out of it. The usefulness lies in how we choose to apply that knowledge.

If we know that most of the activities we engage in don't work, the logical first step to achieving our goals more often is to identify those activities that most often do work.

Defining Your Terms

Just for a minute, let's go back to the day you used in the little mind experiment you conducted at the beginning of this chapter. If you're reading this book, it means that you're committed and dedicated to doing what it takes to get to that Top 5%, so must likely it was a really busy day.

Now that you've read the previous section, it's a pretty sobering thought that there's a very good chance most of what kept you busy that day was just that "busy work." Discovering that you're simply treading water when you think you're winning the race is a good time to reevaluate your stroke.

Voltaire, a great philosopher of the Enlightenment, left us with a great quote when he said, "If you wish to converse with me, define your terms." In other words, you can't talk about – or do anything about – "something" unless you've given definition to that "something." And the something professional sales people are most interested in are prospects most likely to buy – which means the first thing that needs to be done is define the characteristics of prospects most likely to buy from you.

However, defining this "Most Likely to Buy" prospect isn't something you can just pull out of a hat. You're not interested in defining who you think might buy from you. What you want to know is who will buy from you. Therefore, simple logic tells us that the best place to start developing the criteria to qualify a prospective customer is to analyze the characteristics of customers who are currently buying from you.

After identifying who is buying from you, it is time to ferret out shared characteristics. This process can be facilitated by asking some fairly simple questions:

- What accounts closed fastest?

- What accounts had the largest revenue?

- What customers make the most repeat purchases?

- What customers provide the most referrals?

- Are there any common job titles?

- Is there a relationship between size/type/etc. of a company and how fast they closed, how much, or how often they bought?

- Is location a factor?

The Right Tool for the Right Job

Many of you reading this may already be working with a preset qualified lead (prospect) definition tool provided to you by your employer. This tool is most usually developed as a collaborative effort between marketing and sales for the purpose of coming to an agreement as to the criteria a prospect must meet to be considered a "universal lead" within the company. If this is the case, you might think you're off the hook as the work's already been done for you.

If that were true you probably wouldn't be reading this. Think of it this way, if all we needed to do to get a job done was the right tool, hand anyone a torque wrench and they're magically transformed into a master mechanic.

Using a tool to its greatest advantage takes education, practice, and skill. These are all developed over time.

Generally speaking all lead definition tools should have the following in place:

- Provide criteria to assess both implicit and explicit criteria

- Criteria that differentiates between a qualified lead and a highly qualified lead

- Profile of contact (i.e. decision-maker) and company?

- Identifies buying stage and need

- Includes data on recentness, activity/action types, and registrations

Key benefits for developing a qualified lead definition tool include:

- Improve collaboration between marketing and sales

- Generate leads worth investing sales effort and activity

- Increase revenue

Any mechanic or carpenter will tell you having the right tool for the right job is essential. Any customer of that mechanic or carpenter will tell you how that mechanic or carpenter puts that tool into practice is what makes the difference.

Not Every Prospect is a Match

You might think of a qualified lead definition tool as a kind of matchmaking service. Many people include in their reasons for using such a service the fact that they don't have time to waste on dating people that don't meet certain criteria important to them.

Today there's a proliferation of online dating services where you can list the criteria you seek, and the service matches you with people who meet that general criteria. But, just because you've now got a list of people who met your criteria doesn't mean each and every person on that list is your soul mate. Instead, you rank each person on the list as to how closely they meet your criteria and then meet with them individually in order to establish if they are worth investing the time and effort needed to create a successful relationship.

This is almost exactly how a professional sales person uses their qualified lead definition tool. The tool provides you with a list that qualifies the prospect, but it is your job to do work needed to drill down to those prospects that represent the best use of your time.

For example, "need" is certainly going to be included in any criteria for qualifying a prospect. However, there is a whole continuum of "need" that stretches from "we don't need it" to "it would be nice to have" to "we can't survive without it." Additionally, even if the prospect has a need they believe they cannot survive without doesn't mean that the prospect has the budget, or the authority to fill that need.

Top performers understand that an important part of winning means accurately confirming that the criteria that qualified a lead does, in fact, represent a prospect worth investing their time and effort – and they do this early on in the process of authenticating qualified leads. Remember, wasting your time, or your customer's time, is of no value to you or your customer.

Creating Your Own Qualified Lead Definition Tool

Not every professional sales person works within a company that has provided them with a qualified lead definition tool. If that's the case, a top performer's response is taking steps to develop one.

This can be done by following the following steps:

•   Get buy-in and support for the project from key influencers first.

•   Contact marketing and sales directors. Get their cooperation in creating a list of shared characteristics of customers who are buying from your company.

- Meet with marketing and sales. Develop consensus for criteria.

- Create draft criteria for tool.

- Meet to confirm criteria for tool.

- Publish and distribute tool.

- Continue to meet periodically to reevaluate criteria.

Even in today's business environment where leads come in via the internet, it remains true for most of us that not all leads are going to come wrapped up as a nice and tidy qualified lead. A professional sales person is a professional who prospects – and all prospects must be qualified whether they come to you via your company, by referral, or your own personal effort.

Some companies provide resources to qualify leads. If yours isn't one of them, here's a list of helpful resources:

- The usual suspects: Google search, company website, newsletters, press releases, blogs, social networking sites

- Annual Reports

- Professional Associations

- Better Business Bureau

- Local Chambers of Commerce

- Credit bureaus

- Dun & Bradstreet

- Customers of your prospect

- Vendors who serve your prospect

- Trade journals

Calling Your Prospects to Order

A lead ranking system goes a long way when it comes to sifting out not only the most likely prospects – but the most highly qualified prospects. Highly qualified prospects are a "probable sale" versus a "possible sale."

Ranking systems usually employ a points system – the higher the relationship between a particular characteristic of customers who currently buy from you resulted in a sale, the higher the point value of that characteristic.

Here's a simple example:

- Project is funded   5   points

- Project budget in process of being approved   3   points

- Project not budgeted   0   points

- Contact is decision-maker   5   points

- Contact is recommender   3   points

- Contact is influencer   1   points

- Clearly identified need   5   points

- Plans to buy within 3 months   5   points

- Plans to buy within 6 months   3   points

- Plans to buy within 1 year   1   points

- Plans to buy $XX,000   5   points

- Plans to buy less than $X,000   0   points

In this scenario, prospects with a score of 25 or higher are ranked as a highly qualified lead. Leads are pursued according to their ranking.

The Real Story

Once you've identified your high priority prospects, it's time to put the time and effort into getting in front of your contact – which is when you're going to get the "real story" of exactly how – or how not – your prospect fits the criteria for a highly qualified prospect in the real world versus how they ranked off of your qualified lead definition tool. And you're going to do this by asking questions – and then listening very carefully to how they are answered.

Too many sales professionals think this is the time to jump right into presenting their product or solution. It isn't. Initially your goal is to further qualify your prospect.

While every deal is going to have its own specific criteria, at minimum very early on in the process your conversations and communications with your contact must have provided you with the following information:

Who are you really talking to? You may have thought you were dealing with the decision-maker only to find out weeks later that you've been sitting in front of an influencer at best, or someone who "hoped" they'd be able to talk decision-makers into making a purchase. Titles are important, but being in front of a C-level contact is no guarantee. You're also going to want to know if they are the sole decision-makers. Even if you're sitting in front of the CEO who has made it very clear they're the one who signs the check, you don't want to find out months down the road that the decision-maker's process for making the decision is bringing other people on before a final decision is made.

When do they want or need this to happen? If your contact can't provide you with a time frame it's likely that the project is in a conceptual stage. Certainly this doesn't mean slamming any doors, but you will definitely want to consider changing your approach from winning a sale to that of Trusted Advisor. Prospects that have urgent needs and drop-dead time frames are most likely to result in a sale.

Who else are they talking to? What other solutions are they considering? While you're thinking you're qualifying a prospect, your prospect can be thinking they're meeting to discuss just one option among many – and some of those options may not include making a purchase. Be open to discussing whether or not there are solutions available that don't include a purchase from your company.

Of course, you also need to know if they are seeking other bids. If so, an important question to ask is why they are getting other bids. You don't want to discover after you've put your heart and soul into the project that the only reason they wanted your bid is outside bids were required before they could be authorized to purchase from their usual vendor. Not that this means a sale is impossible, but that kind of information is what you need to know in order to continuously prioritize your pipeline.

Additionally you want to ask what it is that will determine a winning bid.

What is motivating them to consider a purchase? Speaking of asking what it is that will make your prospect chose one bid over another – developing a very clear understanding of what is behind your prospects motivation to buy is equally essential. If you don't have this information, you can't customize your sales presentation to your prospect.

What would make them not want to buy from you? Today's economy has wrought a ton of risk aversion and cost cutting. Discovering what would prompt your prospect to back out of a deal or not buy in the first place both acts to assist you in prioritizing your leads, as well as let you know whether you can cover those objections.

You need to have all of the above under your belt in order to properly analyze your prospects true qualifications as a likely buyer. Here are a couple other approaches you may also want to put into practice:

See if a prospect is willing to complete a request you make. If prospect is willing to take some time to provide you with what you've requested, this increases the likelihood that they are seriously interested in making a purchase.

Ask questions designed to see if your company is a good match for the prospect. These questions are of benefit to both you and your prospect. Making sure that you're a good fit means making sure that you can deliver the prospect's expectations. Making sure that you're a good fit also can serve to bring to light any red flags that the prospect's expectations exceed the deal's profitability.

Bring prospects in to meet with your team. This can actually serve to practically make the sale for you. When a prospect meets with your team, this can often result in that prospect behaving as if the sale is already a "done deal" making it a much easier to close the deal.

What Matters When Qualifying a Prospect

According to Bob Apollo, Member of the Harvard Business Review Advisory Council, there are only three things that matter when qualifying your prospect:

- Are they **really** likely to buy?

- Are you **really** likely to win?

- Is it **really** worth the effort?

We couldn't agree more, but want to add these three questions shouldn't only be asked early on in the sales cycle. Each and every time you speak or communicate with a prospect is a good time to ask these three questions one more time.

How you answer them lets you know whether or not to increase your efforts, or back off a bit and use time you would have spent with a stalled customer on a higher ranked prospect.

Post Chapter Exercise:

1. List your qualifying steps:
2. Role-play step #2 with a coworker. Can you determine 100% of the time you are investing your time wisely?
3. What are your "qualifying" elements?

VISION & IMPLICATION

"Top Performers Ask Great Questions"

I am going to start this chapter off by asking you to do something that, although it may sound easy, can be rather difficult. However, unless and until you succeed in accomplishing what you're going to be asked to do, you will never make it to that Top 5% or, if you get lucky

> **Step # 3**
>
> Approach
>
> Discovery
>
> **Vision & Implication**
>
> Solution
>
> Engagement

and meet that lofty goal – it won't be for long. Here's what you need to do:

"Forget all the manipulative techniques you have been taught about selling. ALL of them, they do not work. Instead, practice patience, courtesy – and, above all, ask great questions and be truly interested in what your prospect has to say."

Asking someone to forget something doesn't seem to be too much to ask. We're only human and we forget things all the time. So, forgetting what you've been taught about selling might not seem like such a big deal. But it is, because turning you're back on what you've been taught also means you must stop believing old school manipulative selling works.

Manipulative might seem too strong a word. However, we've already established that traditional sales techniques are all about selling product. Today's customer runs from any sales person whose approach is concentrated on "getting the sale" as this is very easily, and correctly, translated by your customer to mean you're goal is to get them to do something for you (buy from you). Instead of seeing you as someone who can do something for them, your customer sees you as wanting something from them – and then doing your best to talk them into giving it to you. And that smacks of being manipulated.

Furthermore, customers aren't interested in doing you favors, at least not unless you've become a Trusted Advisor. Until you've established yourself as a Trusted Advisor, your customer will always assume your primary goal is to act in your own (and your company's) best interest – and this certainly doesn't provide them with a good reason to buy from you. OK, so old techniques don't work. What does?

Funny you should ask, because the answer to that question is: Asking great questions.

Getting the Sale versus Winning the Sale

There is a huge difference between "getting the sale" and "winning the sale." Getting something doesn't imply there's any discipline, passion, or skill involved – at least none based on integrity and founded on trust. On the other hand, winning a sale implies that much passion, discipline, and skill were applied. Nothing is handed over to us "just because" or due to a person being "led" to buy from you. Instead, the sale was won by becoming a valued Trusted Advisor who always acts in the best interest of the customer.

Think of it this way. For a couple years a high school football team has a less than stellar coach who trains them in techniques to manipulate the rules. Now, they may win a few games that way but, sooner or later, they're going to be penalized and, if they continue to try to win games that way, they will ultimately lose.

But let's say they don't lose and come out at first place in their division at the end of the season. They don't win the state championship, but they feel pretty darn good about their season. Next season rolls around, and the players are pretty confident they can manipulate more wins. However, the refs are now on to them and they begin to lose games and come in last place in their division. At the end of the season the coach is fired.

At the start of the new season their new coach tells them to forget everything they've been taught. Instead, he teaches them not only a respect for the rules, but also shows them how following the rules can actually help them win. The new coach instills in his players a passion for the game along with extensive practice and drilling to improve their skills. It takes them a couple seasons, but the next time they put that first place division trophy in the case, they know it wasn't given to them; they know didn't manipulate the rules to get it. That trophy was earned. And when they run onto the field at the start of that year's state championship – they know they earned the right to be there.

That high school team goes on to become a serious contender always placing in the top five for years to come.

Similarly, the Top 5% sales professionals understand that they must "earn the right" in order to win the sale. They aren't out there selling single transactions based on features, benefits, or (huge mistake) price.

How Do You Rank?

24% of sales people today only sell features & benefits. This is the least effective means to win the sale.

56% sell solutions. They ask a few good questions and are

primarily just focused on the single transaction.

15% of sales people are working at not pushing product and instead become very good at asking questions and advising clients. Their focus is slowly changing to ask good questions and present solutions that help the customer's customer.

The Top 5% of sales professionals ask great questions. They are a Trusted Advisor, serving as the customer's consultant. They typically practice the 10-90-10 principle with 10% of their time spent asking questions; 90% of their time intently listening for understanding of what is being said to them; and 10% of their time spent presenting the solution.

How to Become a Trusted Advisor

Since this chapter is all about how important it is to ask questions in order to win the sale, we'll start this section with a very important question to ask yourself:

Would a customer pull out a checkbook and compensate me just for the sales call?

If your answer would typically be "No" – you might be wondering "Why?" - especially if you hold yourself as relatively skilled when it comes to communicating value. The answer is that business-to-business sales professionals must actually create value, not just communicate value.

So, how do you create that value? Fortunately, you don't have to create the wheel when it comes to figuring out how to bring real value for your customer. Simply examining what Highly Successful Top 5% performers do every day provides an excellent road map for creating value.

Get in the Game. The highly successful professional sales person maximizes their value by learning everything there is to know about their customer's business.

Work Backward. In order to provide meaningful solutions Top Percenters continuously reexamine their customer's vision and then work backward to produce solutions that support that vision.

Adopt a Routine. If there is one thing you've got to have in place to become both a Top Performer as well as a Trusted Advisor that has to be implementing a planned sales process. Purposeful sales processes can be measured and duplicated over and over again with consistent results. The only way to implement an effective sales process is to adopt a daily routine; and the only way to become a Trusted Advisor is be certain your process and routine includes scheduling time in your day to study your customers.

Ask A LOT of Questions. We'll talk more about what questions to ask. For now, understand that highly successful sales professionals ask a lot of questions. Generally speaking, effective questions are based on information gleaned by researching the customer. Questions let the customer know you are there to serve their best interests and establish credibility needed to "Earn the Right" to be their Trusted Advisor.

You can't create value by deciding for your customer what those values might be. Sales people become Trusted Advisors when they can give their customers ideas about their business that they didn't come up with themselves. Certainly you want to be able to offer your customer solutions or tactics they may not have considered if not for your insight. However, the value you bring to your customers must be both useful and meaningful to them. How you discover ideas that will be of value to your customer is by asking great questions, listening intently, and then providing your customer with meaningful, useful solutions.

You may consider yourself to be a Trusted Advisor to a number of your customers. If so, you should be able to answer the following questions about each of those customers:

- What is the problem that my company solves better than our competitors?

- How effective am I in my questioning process to help identify latent pains points my customer experiences?

- Have I identified and do I fully understand my customer's "drivers"?

What's Driving Your Customer?

For a mechanical engineer, a driver is "a part of a machine that causes another part to move." A driver can also be a tool, such as a drill, "that exerts heavy pressure on something else."

For a professional sales person, what's driving your customer is

anything that causes them to take a particular action or any situation or circumstance that is causing a problem and/or requires action. Knowing what's driving your customer provides you with the information you need in order to create real value and become a Trusted Advisor to your customer. Attempting to create a relationship of trust by coming in and attempting to "help" your customer by identifying their drivers for them falls back on outdated techniques designed to convince a customer that they've got problems or needs your product can meet and solve. Your research, along with careful questioning may reveal a driver(s) your customer has not considered. When this is the case, ask incrementally more specific questions regarding that driver rather than "informing" your customer they have overlooked an important factor.

Your customer is likely to view you as driven mainly by the desire to make the sale. A great way to see how important asking questions that identify your customer's drivers is by reviewing questions your customer is likely asking themselves about you:

• Does this sales person truly understand my problem and the cause?

• Is this (situation, circumstance, product, service, etc.) worth changing?

• Does this sales person understand how our entire organization is affected?

• Does this sales person truly have a solution or directly address this issue?

• Do I want to put my reputation on the line and move this process forward?

If your customer's answers to all the above is "Yes" – instead of seeing you as a "product pusher", you are on your way to becoming your customer's Trusted Advisor who will win the sale when your customer's needs and/or problems have a match in the services and/or products your company offers. However, in order for you to behave in a manner that provides your customer with a meaningful value, you've got to understand exactly what's driving your customer.

There are different types of customer drivers:

- **Financial Drivers** are related to producing profit.

- **Operational Drivers** are concerned with how the customer can improve their organization.

- **Supplier Drivers** revolve around the reliability of supply, quality, and economies of scale.

- **Customer Drivers** are solutions that successfully retain and grow your customer's customer base.

- **Competitor Drivers** are related to keeping the competition at bay.

- **Regulatory Drivers** represent the ability to maintain compliance with government, agency, and professional regulations.

- **Personal Drivers** relate to the customer's ego, self-esteem, and desire to fulfill personal achievement goals.

Before You Ask – Learn to Listen

It is a common stereotype to think that sales people talk too much. It is also unfortunately too often all too true. As a matter-of-fact, you can probably recall quite a few times when you left a presentation or ended a sales call knowing that you'd talked too much – enough that might have put you out of the running to either win the sale or done anything to establish the trust and credibility needed for your customer to consider you their Trusted Advisor. Walking back to your car, or snapping your cell phone shut you might have thought, "Why did I talk too much?" Some pretty common reasons include:

• Fear of losing control of the sales call or presentation.

• No prepared, strategic outlook because you didn't know your customer or their vision well enough – just "pushing product."

• The customer wasn't talking; you were just filling in the silence.

• Your style is more to "wing it."

• You weren't prepared to match any of your competitive advantages and needed to redirect and "fill in" the conversation.

Any of the above means you most likely wasted your time as well as your customer's. Asking great questions based on researching your customer and geared towards understanding their drivers is a much better use of time – one that provides a greater return on investing that time for both you and your customer. However, asking questions is actually less than half of the equation.

In their book "Conceptual Selling" Stephen Heiman and Robert Miller identify three phases of any sales call – and only one-third of this very successful process involves the sales person uttering a word.

- Phase One: Getting Information – Sales person listening 70% of the time.

- Phase Two: Giving Information – Sales person listening 30% of the time.

- Phase Three: Getting Commitment – Sales person listening 50% of the time.

Top performing sales professionals aren't known for their ability to speak nonstop. Instead they are known for their ability to listen. The best sales people understand the importance of listening. They are great listeners. They are acutely aware of the importance of practicing good listening skills as they understand effective selling depends upon mastering the art of being able to establish a dialogue – not an ability to speak indefinitely or "talk the customer" into buying. They know the most successful means to establish dialogue with customers is to ask questions.

Before You Ask - Practice Patience

At the beginning of this chapter you were told to forget everything you'd been taught about selling and for most sales professionals this means learning new skills. Whenever we learn new skills we tend to make mistakes at first and learning to sell by establishing a dialogue with your customer by asking questions certainly isn't an exception to that trend.

There are some pretty common pitfalls when first implementing questions based dialogue with your customer. Knowing what they are is the first step to avoiding them:

• Shooting yourself in the foot by asking rapid fire questions, one right after another. It is a dialogue – not an interrogation.

• Not waiting for, or giving your customer enough time to answer questions. Studies have shown that people often wait less than one second before starting to answer or respond. There is no better way to demonstrate that you aren't listening before you respond, which is interpreted as your having very little interest in what is being said to you.

• Moving on to the next question or topic before your customer is ready. You may think you've got enough information, but your customer just might have a few facts, feelings, or data necessary for you to fully understand their needs, problems, or drivers. Again, you cannot assume you know enough to be of value to your customer. Instead, check in with your customer before moving the conversation forward by asking a related question.

• You are not a parrot. Forget about "repeating back" exactly what your customer says to you. This can be a very annoying and obvious technique. Instead, if you need clarification, ask for it. When you want to be absolutely certain you fully understand what your customer is telling you, relay to the customer your understanding of what they just said to you – again, in the form of a question.

•   Never ask your customer to "Think about it." You are not a mind reader and can't get information from people's thoughts – you need them to tell you their thoughts. If a customer doesn't have an answer to your question at the time you ask, let them know you can return to the topic at a later date and make arrangements before the conversation is over to contact them again to discuss it further.

•   Remove the phrase "Yes...but" from your conversational repertoire, it will only get you into trouble. You don't want to appear to have taken offense to what has been said or put into a position where you appear to be "defending" your company, your product, or yourself from attack. When you feel a "Yes... but" coming on, ask a related clarifying or open-ended question instead.

•   Outside of listening itself, your greatest ally for effectively using questions to establish dialogue is patience, and patience requires discipline. Sometimes silence truly is golden and allowing what may first be an uncomfortable "golden silence" into play is what you need to get a meaningful answer from your customer. Don't be afraid to ask a question, shut your mouth, and wait for an answer. Give your customer the courtesy of allowing them time to think it through.

Asking the Right Customer the Right Questions

Remember that asking great questions is a wise use of both your time and your client's time – and the best way to waste both party's time is pursuing an improperly or unqualified customer. This does not mean if you determine that your customer isn't ready to buy now that asking them questions is a waste of time.

Instead you can think of "qualifying" a customer as a means to prioritize your time. This is done by finding answers to the following seven questions:

- Is it budgeted?

- What is the application?

- How much do they need?

- Who is the competition?

- Target price?

- When do they need it?

- Why would they buy from me? (Value proposition)

If you've got definitive answers for at least four of the above – you've qualified your customer. Use the specifics of those answers to prioritize how much time to spend on particular customers based on the expected return. For example, two qualified customers have a need that will take place in six months. Customer "A" is most likely a one-time, low budget purchase. Customer "B" is a repeat customer experiencing business growth who will likely be making similar future cyclical purchases. You don't ignore Customer "A", but plan to spend more time on Customer "B".

But What Kinds of Questions Should I Ask?

The only way you were able to determine how to prioritize Customer "A" and Customer "B" is by asking questions that elicit the customer's short-term needs along with their long-term strategies as well as questions that reveal problems a customer is trying to either "fix" or "avoid."

Asking the right questions reveals the customer's buying criteria that (eventually) leads to a profitable sale and partnership.

But you don't just "jump in" and start asking questions. It doesn't take an M.B.A. to understand why – all you have to do is walk a mile in your prospect's shoes. Let's turn the tables and imagine a new prospect calls and makes an appointment with you. Before you've even had time to sit back down in your chair after greeting them, your new customer starts asking you very probing questions regarding intimate (and even proprietary) questions about you and your company. You don't even know this person, how can you trust them with that kind of information?

Trust is something that is built, question-by-question, answer by answer starting with broad questions and then drilling down to specifics. A general outline of this progression is as follows:

1.   General business questions related to the industry.

2.   Specific business questions related to the specific customer.

3.   Specific business questions that lead to your company's competitive advantages.

Understanding the progression is one thing, but what topics do you use to design the questions themselves? Not surprisingly, questions are designed around the very topics we've been discussing:

•   Questions related to your research on the customer's company.

•   Questions related to your customer's drivers.

•   Questions that qualify the opportunity.

•   Questions that establish the buying criteria.

In 1987, studying the model, "Conceptual Selling" (Miller/ Heiman 2002) we learned these topics are then broken down even further into five specific types of questions that can be asked for each topical area:

1.   **Confirmation Question** - These questions are asked in order to confirm specific information and data collected when researching your customer and their company.

2.   **New Information Request** - We've all experienced "gaps" that need to be addressed in order to properly design an offering that meets the customer's needs and/or solves their problems - asking questions that reveal new information is how to fill those gaps.

3.   **Commitment Questions** - Again, your time is as valuable as your customer's. Questions designed to assess your customer's willingness to take next steps in the buying process are absolutely necessary and should be asked throughout the sales process as a means to continuously qualify and prioritize time spent on the customer.

4.   **General Questions** - These questions are designed to help uncover potential concerns that can derail the sale. The answers to these questions provide the most definitive answer(s) to the underlying concern "What would make you not buy from me?"

5.   **Attitude Questions** - This type of question deserves its own section – which is coming right up. Generally speaking, attitude questions are those designed to uncover the customer's true and most influential needs, values, and attitudes.

But, before we move on, we need to get all the cards on the table – in particular, let's talk about price. Your Average Joe or Joanne sales person usually sticks to selling on price. Big mistake. Quite often this is the case due to a false fear that the only thing the customer is interested in is buying based on price.

This assumption will always backfire. When the sales person focuses on price, that's where you place the customer's focus as well. When that happens, you find yourself in a situation where the customer misperceives your offering as only price based – or worse, too expensive.

There are customers who come into the sales conversation intending to base their buying decision on price. The reason for this is that this type of customer perceives there IS no additional value. Asking great questions is the only way to discover areas even the customer isn't aware of that reveal additional value when buying from you.

And then there are customers (about 30 to 40%) who buy based on price and, no matter what, will always buy based on price. If you're a "cup half full" kind of thinker, your first reaction is to fear losing that 30-40%. On the other hand, if you think like a Top Performer, this is great news because that means 60-70% of your target buy based on value.

When your sales questions, calls, and presentations focus on value along with credible offers of assistance and solutions for your customer's current and future challenges, you create a Trusted Advisor relationship where that customer will come to view a buying relationship with you as an investment in solving their problems. Sell value and you may never be the lowest price, but you will always be the lowest cost because you represent the highest value to your customer.

Attitude is Everything

Attitude questions surface gaps in your information about the one thing that drives the sale – the client's mental picture of what buying from you can do for him. Remember that if the results define what he buys, values and attitudes define why. (Emphasis mine)" – *Miller/ Heiman*

No matter how authentic a relationship, WIFM (What's in it for me) always applies. In true partnerships, WIFM is always win-win. However, in order for the relationship to be authentic, you must first establish the values and attitudes that truly drive your customer's intention to buy – or not buy – from you.

Attitude questions might seem to be a bit tricky to both design as well as ask. However, the opposite is actually true. Rather than resent being asked for their personal opinion, or how something may or may not have an impact on them – customer's usually appreciate the opportunity to be heard. And attitude questions don't have to be invasive. When asking attitude questions use the same model of asking broad questions and then drilling down to specifics should be followed. This pattern of questioning builds trust incrementally.

Asking attitude questions doesn't have to be hard. Here are a few intro's you can use to practice asking them:

• What is your opinion about (fill in the blank)?

- How might (insert what will change) impact you?

- What would (insert your solution) mean to you personally?

Strategy and Sequencing Count

Jumping in with invasive questions can certainly stall building trust in a relationship. So can jumping around asking seemingly random, unrelated questions. Doing so hardly builds credibility with your customer. Instead you might appear to be floundering aimlessly about, hoping you'll eventually hit a target that means something to your client.

Asking your customer questions isn't a more grown up version of wandering about trying to pin the tail on the donkey. Instead, asking great questions means asking strategic questions designed to create a dialogue that qualifies your customers, uncovers gaps, engenders credibility, and builds trust.

Marc Miller's book "A Seat at the Table" (Miller, 2010) introduced some very powerful questioning techniques. Of particular interest is his F.O.C.A.S. technique, an excellent strategy for designing questions that create value for your customer. This method is true to its name, and provides a framework to develop clearly focused, revealing questions.

Fact Questions - These are questions that explore important facts or data that describe the customer's current situation. These are extremely useful, but caution must be taken not to ask too many or too long questions as well as questions that are excessively tactical in nature.

Objective Questions - This type of question explores your prospect's objectives and opportunities and is extremely useful for facilitating the business conversation. The questions you ask should align with your company's competitive advantages. Although tempting, be sure not to ask too many questions to elicit pain points – instead concentrate on your customer's vision. Remember, you want to be able to "work backwards" from the customer's vision in order to provide solutions that support that vision.

Concern Questions - These questions explore your customer's strategic problems. Properly designed, this type of questioning has a high payoff as they lay the groundwork to build your case for change. Remember, you are discussing the customer's difficulties, concerns, challenges, and problems. This type of question must always be well considered, well researched, and well prepared.

Anchor Questions - Miller suggests you "drop anchor" on areas that concern your customer and/or are problems for your client. Exploring the consequences of these concerns and problems by asking questions that relate to those concerns and problems helps your customer connect them to ineffective strategy or tactics – you further assist the client by providing solutions. You may even uncover other areas your company could provide strategic value. But it is important to be patient, don't rush into the solution until your case for change is fully understood and acknowledged.

Solution Questions - These are questions that more fully explore the potential value your solution provides your customer. Instead of "teaching" or "pointing out" that value, ask questions that serve to reveal that value to your customer. For Example: "What percentage of an increase in production would that represent?"

The sequencing of these types of questions is also important. Your doctor doesn't prescribe medication prior to making a diagnosis. And that diagnosis starts by asking the patient questions. Questions that are asked in specific sequences based on the patient's answers.

The power of F.O.C.A.S. is that is provides a framework for sequencing progression of the business conversation. No more trying to pin the tail on the donkey. Instead, practice first asking diagnostic questions, anchor revealed concerns with impact questions, and then follow up with solution questions.

If you were to map out the sequencing for effective questions that elicit meaningful dialogue with your customer that leads to winning the sale and help establish you as a Trusted Advisor it would look something like this:

Diagnostic?

- Fact?

- Objective?

Impact?

- Concern?

- Anchor?

Solution?

- Solution

We'll end this chapter where we began:

"Forget all the manipulative techniques you have been taught about selling. ALL of them, they do not work. Instead, practice patience, courtesy – and, above all, ask great questions and be truly interested in what your prospect has to say."

If your vision is to become, or maintain your status, as a Top 5% (or 1%, like Mr. Trump says, "you might as well think big") performer, take the above as your mantra and make it your mission to incorporate asking great questions into your sales process.

Post Chapter Exercise:

1. Why do traditional sales people fail?

2. Why do sales people talk too much?   What are some techniques to correct?

3. What are your "main" goals when making a sales call?

4. Name 5 question types and there importance.

5. Consider an upcoming key sales presentation. Can you develop 1-3 questions that will facilitate the business conversation that needs to take place?

6. Create three fact questions and three attitude questions that will focus on learning more about your customers business.

7. Consider the problems that your product or service can solve. Now develop a list of concern questions followed up by anchor questions.

SOLUTION

Rock climbing can teach you a lot about sales.

First and foremost, you've got to have a passion for climbing

rocks.   And, similar to sales, rock
climbing is a process. You need to
trust that you're healthy and
possess the strength, and
endurance to make the climb. You
must perform research in order to
qualify what level of difficulty the
unique place you've chosen to
make your climb represents. You

Step # 4

Approach

Discovery

Vision & Implication

Solution

Engagement

need to analyze what problems you're likely to face and plan
what personal strengths and skills you can leverage to provide
solutions for those problems.

You need to decide what gear you'll need and, if you don't have
what you need, assess the particular features and benefits that
will meet the specific needs of the climb. You must have done
the work needed to train and then have regularly practiced the
skills and techniques necessary to perform successful climbs.

You need to plan your route. You'll want to envision and tell yourself stories of past climbs you've made that lead you to the firm belief that you will be able to do what you need to do in order to solve problems. You'll want to learn from the stories of others.

However, the most important part of the rock climbing process is to review where you're at with all the above before you even think about starting your assent. Your life can literally depend on knowing where you are at any given time.

What does any of this have to do with the sales process?

Not knowing where you're at before moving forward to presenting a solution to your customer can literally kill any hope of winning the sale.

Rock climbing has to be a process, specifically a process that works and can be duplicated, because you've got to know that you will consistently do things right. You need to be taught and engage in a series of actions that will consistently produce the results you seek (not falling).

Sales professionals need to engage in a process that can be duplicated and, when consistently performed, consistently produce the results top performers seek (winning more sales).

The Rules of Results

The following rules are adapted from "Play to Win: Choosing Growth Over Fear in Work and Life" by Larry Wilson and Hersch Wilson (Wilson, 1998).

1.   You cannot control the results you get, but you can influence the results you get.

2.   The results you are getting are the results you should be getting.

3.   If you want different results you have to do something different.

Rule #3 is perhaps the most important of these rules, but let's first throw out a couple insights as to how the first two apply to winning sales.

Rule #1 states a hard, but very true, fact of life. There are things we cannot control. But this rule certainly doesn't leave us dead in the water when it comes to achieving our objectives. Understanding that there are things that will simply be out of our control and the best we can do is bring our influence to bear can make or break a sales professional because it is this understanding that both gets us through unavoidable rejection as well as motivates us to get right back on the horse.

But Rule #1 doesn't let us off the hook. Although there are things we can't control, it is up to us to bring our influence to bear when striving to achieve a particular result. And our influence as sales professionals is delivered by having a planned process in place.

Rule #2 sounds equally harsh, but serves us well. We already know from Rule #1 that we're responsible to bring our influence to bear to get the results we want. It follows that whatever it is that we are consistently doing is what is providing us with those results. More important, it follows that we, and only we, are responsible for those results. This rule is comforting to apply to ourselves when we win – not so much when we lose.

At first Rule #2 may seem to negate Rule #1. If there are things that are out of our control, how can we be responsible for negative results? Let's say you don't win a sale because your prospect buys based solely on price. No matter how much time and effort you spent (and wasted) on bringing your influence to bear it won't (and never will) make any difference to a buyer who bases their decision on price alone. You just don't have that kind of control over how people operate; if the buyer sees no other advantage to choosing to buy from you unless you're the lowest price – you're out.

Here's where the "you're still responsible" for the results you get part comes in: If you identify that you've got a buyer who makes their buying decision based solely on price but keep hammering on that prospect and others like them instead of using that time to find qualified buyers – well, you've got no one to blame but yourself when you don't meet quota.

And this brings us to very important Rule #3. If you're not meeting quota, if you don't have enough opportunities of value coming down the pike you already know Rule #2 tells you that these are the results you should be getting. Of COURSE you want different results. And here is the beauty of Rule #3: Number Three tells you that if you want different results what you need to do is start doing things differently.

Jumping the Gun

There is no other sales professional who needs to "get" The Rules of Results more than a sales person who consistently jumps the gun and confuses "getting the meeting" with a qualified prospect as the perfect time to present their product or solution.

Which brings us right back to how important it is for a sales professional to assess where they are at with a client at any given time, and the way to measure that is by checking to see where you are in terms of your process and your plan.

This chapter isn't meant to be a full review of process or plan; however, hopefully we've made our point in a Big Way:

You need to know where you're at before taking the next step.

Generally speaking, you're not ready to provide a solution and/or make a sales presentation to a customer until:

1.   You have a consistent, measurable, process that has demonstrated the ability to produce consistently positive results in place.

2.   You have created a disciplined plan to follow that process that includes regular and habitual monitoring and assessment.

3.   You've identified and qualified the prospect as high value, high probability by doing the necessary "homework" and "leg work."

4.   You've done the work to earn the right, and are on your way or have already established yourself as a credible expert, and (most of all) Trusted Advisor.

5.   You've asked the prospect the right questions in order to accomplish the following: Determine if you're talking to the right person (i.e. decision-maker or influencer); identify your prospect's problems and uncover any gaps; establish buying criteria.

6.   You've determined your company's "leverage-able" competitive advantages that meet the prospects unique and

specific needs and / or solve their unique and specific problems.

7.   You are able to provide answers to the following questions:

- Do I know who I'm really talking to?

- Do I know when this prospect wants or needs this to happen?

- Do I know who else they are talking to?

- Do I know what other solutions they are considering?

- Do I know what's motivating them to make a purchase?

- Do I know what would make them not buy from me?

Do You Know Where You're Going?

After answering those six questions you've identified where you're at and certain that you know where you're going: You're going to make a solution/sales presentation to your qualified prospect.

Again, let's make absolutely sure you don't jump the gun by giving you a few questions to ask yourself before you take the plunge:

- Do I know what kind of presentation I should make?

- What is the goal of my presentation?

- What objective do I seek to meet as a result of my

presentation?

- What strategies should I employ?

- Do I know how to use effective presentation techniques?

- Do I know what mistakes to avoid?

A quick review of these questions is probably enough to get your heart racing – but they aren't meant to make you nervous, they're meant to help you prepare. Once you're able to answer those questions confidently, you'll be chomping at the bit to get in front of your prospect and ready to WOW them.

The WOW Factor

Before we give you some important guidelines for answering those potentially nerve racking questions, here are nine simple suggestions for "How to WOW Your Prospect" when making your presentation – following them practically guarantees being able to lower your blood pressure when you walk in the room.

1.   Don't pretend you're something you're not. Remember when you were so nervous on your first date or job interview? Much of that nervousness likely stemmed from attempting to impersonate someone you thought would impress your date or interviewer instead of "being yourself."

2.   Get to know everyone. It is likely that you might be presenting to more than one person and equally likely that you won't know all of them. Take a few minutes (key word: few) and invite participants to give a quick 30-second elevator speech as to who they are and what they bring to the table. Use your judgment, but after you've listened to their elevator speech this can be a good time to ask a question or two to help you anticipate individual objections (Caution: make sure your questions are very general, now is NOT the time to attempt to cover objections.)

3.   Keep no secrets. The number one secret you never want to keep is the fact that you don't know an answer to a question. If you don't know, say so, let the asker know you will find out, and provide a date you will get back to the individual or group with the answer. If you don't have the answer by the specified date, determine when you can expect one, and then update your prospect(s).

You also don't want to keep any secrets regarding key deliverables (i.e. timeframe, scope).   Pretending you're something you're not is always a mistake – so is pretending your company, products, and/or services is something they're not is an even bigger (and usually fatal) mistake. And "pretending by omission" counts as keeping a secret.

4.   Make it interactive. Productive presentations are not one-way lectures or tutorials. For example, in order for you to know whether or not you've gained commitment you will need to build in time to interact with your prospect(s.) Depending on the complexity of the sale this might simply be by providing time for "Q and A" at the end of the presentation – or you may want to interact at key points in your presentation.

5.   Keep it simple. To paraphrase Occam's Razor, "The simplest solution is usually the best." Same goes for solution/sales presentations.

6.   Know your material. This cannot be emphasized enough. "Know your material" doesn't only mean practicing your presentation until it comes naturally, it also means being absolutely certain that you have made your absolute best effort to have expert command of your solution, products, and services – as well as an equal command of all the pertinent information you collected from your client by asking the right questions and via data you have collected about your prospect, their company, their industry sector, and other factors that influence the buying decision.

Knowing your material helps you avoid feeling you're up there performing a rendition of Abbott and Costello's "Who's on First?" routine. But again, if you don't know something, don't keep it a secret.

7.   Have answers to objections ready. Many presentations include being able to anticipate "usual suspect" objections that you hear from most prospects. However, resist the temptation to cover those objections with "usual suspect" responses. Instead, craft a response that resonates with the prospect you are in front of.

If you're ready to make a solution/sales presentation, we've already seen that means you've asked the right questions. Asking the right questions most usually includes answers that uncover objections. Prepare for them before making your presentation. Again, use your judgment. Sometimes covering an objection in your presentation works very well, but it can also open a can of worms you'd rather address once your presentation is complete. The point is: Be ready.

8.   Know your commitment action. Remember the old American Express Card ad "Don't leave home without it"? Don't leave home without knowing your commitment action. Your commitment action depends on factors such as what type of presentation you are making (more on that later), the buying cycle, who decision makers are, time frames, etcetera and can range from "getting the check signed" to getting the prospect to commit to a second meeting. Certainly there will be circumstances where you'll want to have more than one commitment action up your sleeve to keep the ball rolling with a high quality, high probability prospect.

Obtaining "commitment" from your prospect indicates that they are involved and moving forward with you towards accepting your solution - and your winning the sale.

9.   Practice – Practice – Practice. In order to "be yourself" when making a solution/sales presentation you must be completely comfortable delivering it. The only way to achieve the needed level of comfort is to practice. Practice in front of a mirror. Practice into an audio recorder. Practice in front of a camcorder. Practice in front of trusted friends and colleagues. Practice, and then practice again, and again. Your presentation should come as naturally to you as if you were talking to a group of well-known colleagues at an informal lunch meeting. You'll know you're ready when you feel absolutely prepared, but your presentation doesn't appear, or sound, "canned."

In particular, you want to "know your intro" backwards and forwards. Not only will this set the tone and WOW your prospect, when you're intro goes smoothly you'll get a rapid injection of confidence to carry with you throughout your presentation.

What Kind of Presentation are You Making?

It would seem the answer to the question "what kind" of presentation you'll be making is rather obvious: You're going to present either a product or service where you'll include the competitive advantages of your product or service that meets the need(s) and/or solve a problem(s) for your prospect in ways that fulfill their buying criteria as well as bring more meaningful value to your prospect than what the competition offers. You are there to win the sale.

Not necessarily. Remember the importance of knowing where you are at throughout the process. There are two types of presentations:

- Introduction of your company

- Solution Presentation

Introducing Your Company

This type of presentation is most often used to gain credibility as well as earn the right. It can be thought of as a more formal way to present your company and its products and/services, in a manner that increases trust between you, your prospect, and your company than you provided when arranging the opportunity to present. However, never forget introducing your company does not mean "pushing product."

Top performers routinely have multiple meetings where they ask the right questions in order to determine solutions specific to their prospect. In other words, this presentation is not an offering, nor is the objective (necessarily) to close the sale (but this does happen, so be prepared). Instead, the "Introduction to My Company" presentation is the time to present general recommendations.

For instance, if you haven't had the opportunity to ask the right questions, you can use this presentation to introduce how your company has provided industry specific solutions. This is where honing your ability to tell "stories" comes into play. Once you've shared general recommendations as well as stories as to how your company's offerings have provided viable solutions, you can then stimulate a very powerful business conversation by asking questions and then listening very carefully to your prospect's answers as they allow you to further "diagnose" your prospect's gaps and/or problems. You then use your prospect's answers to generate a follow up meeting to discuss specific solutions.

Solution Presentation

Now is a good time to remember how we started this chapter – we emphasized the profound importance of knowing where you're at before making a next step. It is imperative that you not attempt to provide a solution until and unless you have properly diagnosed your prospect's gaps or problems and have conducted in depth business conversation(s) with your prospect. Certainly a solution presentation may be possible during the initial sales call depending on complexity. However, solution presentations are usually not made until a minimum of a second or third sales call.

Solution presentations are organized around competitive advantage and it is most usually impossible to identify what competitive advantages to leverage with specific clients until and unless you are certain you "are there" as we've described in this chapter.

As a matter-of-fact, attempting to present a solution preemptively can serve to alienate your prospect and cause them to lose trust. This is easy to understand if you just walk a mile in their shoes. It does seem arrogant to assume that you have the solution to your prospect's problem when they haven't fully disclosed their problems to you. Prospects come to trust you when they know serving their best interest is your prime motivator. Attempting to sell a solution before a prospect has come to trust you enough to disclose tells them what you are interested in is closing a sale.

What is the Goal of My Presentation?

Once again we appear to be asking the obvious. The ultimate goal of making a solution or sales presentation is, of course, to make or win the sale. Or is it?

Even if you are able to win the sale as the result of your "Introduce My Company" or "Solution" presentation you will never win a long-term customer unless your goal is to present a win-win solution.

By definition win-win means that there is something in it for all parties. This means that your company and your company's products or services must be a good fit for your client. Don't try to marry the prince by forcing the shoe to fit – it never works in the long haul. If you aren't a good fit, thank them and be ready to walk away, but maybe not forever. Asking the right questions means you can determine whether the prospect remains a high value, high probability prospect for future business. If that is the case, you're on your to achieve your long-term goal of becoming Trusted Advisor to your prospect – and that's definitely a win-win solution.

What is the Objective of My Presentation?

No matter which type of presentation, be it either introducing your company or presenting a solution, top performers are clear as to objectives that must be met in order to continue to consider the prospect a viable opportunity.

Primary Objective

This is the most optimal result of the presentation. Sure, it is a given that winning the sale is always the most optimal result anytime you interact with a customer or prospect. But, again, unless you're certain this is definitely where you're at (see "Jumping the Gun"), a good process to determine your primary objective is to ask yourself:

- What needs to happen before I can win this sale?

- What do I need to know in order to win this sale?

For example, if you're introducing your company after a general face-to-face or phone discussion with a new high value or high probability prospect, you know "what" absolutely must happen is to gain the trust of your prospect. Now you need to set an objective along with tactics you'll use as the "how" to gain the trust of your prospect.

For instance, you may ask for some data regarding the prospects goals and objectives in order to investigate possible solutions (even if it is a solution outside the scope of your offering, this is how you gain trust). If your prospect is willing to share data with you (especially if proprietary) you know that you've taken a giant step towards becoming a Trusted Advisor to your prospect and are on the road to winning a future sale.

Secondary Objective

It follows that secondary objectives are the second best optimal result of your presentation. Let's say that you know you need to gain trust, but your prospect wasn't ready to let go of any actual data or proprietary information. It may seem that you've "failed", but actually this is good information as it lets you know where you're at with your prospect. Since you can see they don't trust you enough yet to give you the information you can be pretty certain you haven't yet established your credentials as an expert. Instead of using your prospects specific data, you can instead discuss bringing back high level industry specific information and set the appointment to do that.

A secondary objective of any presentation is covering any objections that come up. And, because you've done the work needed to WOW your prospect, you're already prepared to cover "usual suspect" objections customized to the prospect you're in front of. However, we all know that you've got a pretty good opportunity to meet up with an objection you can't cover right then because you don't have enough information, or you simply "don't know." So, secondary objectives also often include arranging a follow up meeting after you've done your homework.

Tertiary Objective

Sometimes, even though you've done your due diligence, followed your process and your plan, and have determined where you're at before putting your presentation together, once you're in front of the prospect you quickly realize you definitely aren't where you thought you were.

For example, your prospect isn't ready to share any information, and they don't seem too interested in having you come back with expert information. You better have a third objective up your sleeve, or there's a good chance you'll find yourself dead the water. Most often this happens because the prospect either held back information when you were in the process of qualifying them by asking great questions or maybe your questions weren't that great.

In our chapter "Top Performers Ask Great Questions" we noted three questions Bob Apollo advises you must be able to answer with a definite "Yes" in order to consider a prospect to be qualified:

- Are the really likely to buy?

- Are you really likely to win?

- Is it really worth the effort?

When you find yourself unable to meet your primary or secondary objective(s) – that's are really good time to quickly run through those questions again using what's happened during your presentation and to determine if your answers are all still "yes."

If your answers aren't a yes, then it may be time to walk. Remember, you don't want to waste your own time, and you don't want to get a reputation for wasting your prospect's time either. On the other hand, if running those questions through another cycle stimulates more qualifying questions you now realize you didn't have answers to, it can be a great time to ask them or set up a follow up meeting with the prospect for that purpose.

Of course, there is another determining factor that you've got to consider alongside setting objectives for your presentation, and that is strategy.

What Strategies Should I Employ?

Before we talk about what strategy you want to use in your

presentation, let's first review some important definitions within the scope of using strategy to create successful plans.

The problem is that it is easy to get the terms confused. For instance, a strategy is not an objective.

The easiest way to tell the difference between a strategy and an objective is that you can measure an objective, whereas strategies are usually very difficult to measure as they are more subjective. For instance, a strategy to win the sale is to earn your customer or prospect's trust. Now, you may have indications that your prospect trusts you, but there is no tape measure you can pull out to verify the "amount" of trust. In other words, it is extremely difficult, if not impossible, to objectively quantify trust.

On the other hand, you can easily measure an objective. For example, you set as your primary objective for your "Introduction to My Company" presentation as having your prospect share data with you that will help you identify any gaps as well as construct useful solutions. You "measure" whether you achieve this objective by whether or not you walk out with the data. It might seem this can't be measured mathematically, but it can. If "Getting Data" equals "1" and "Not Getting Data" equals "2", you either walk out of the presentation with either a 1 or a 2.

We can also confuse a tactic with a strategy. But they are also pretty easy to tell apart because a strategy is the "what" and a tactic is the "how."

For example, when you set your primary objective for your "Introduction to My Company" presentation to be having your prospect trust you with information, "earning my prospect's trust" is a strategy because it is "what" you want to happen. So the question becomes "how" to earn their trust. One tactic, or "how", is to respect the confidentiality of the information they provide you with as well as use that information to provide them with expert advice and meaningful solutions.

A goal is also often confused with strategy and objective.

Goals are long-term, immeasurable aims, whereas we know you can measure objectives. A goal is a sort of "mini-strategy" because they describe a "what" you want to happen related to your strategy. You can think of strategy as a "50,000 Foot What" and a goal as a "25,000 Foot What."

It is easy to see why people can confuse the terms strategy, goal, objective, and tactic. Here is a very simple breakdown using our "Introduction to My Company" example that makes the differences very clear:

Strategy: Earn customer's trust (What you want to happen)

Goal: Become Trusted Advisor (Long-term immeasurable what)

Objective: Obtain data (Measurable objective, you "do" or you "don't")

Tactic: Use data obtained from prospect to uncover gaps and create solutions. Respect confidentiality of data ("How" you earn customer's trust to reach long-term aim of becoming customer's Trusted Advisor)

Whew! Now that we've got all that under our belts, we can turn our attention to specific presentation strategies.

First to Engage Strategy: If you are the first to present to your prospect, your strategy (what you want to happen) is to set the criteria for the sale. This strategy is very powerful as, when you set the criteria, anyone coming after you needs to be able to show they are a match to the criteria you've set. This strategy makes you a "tough act to follow." For example, there is a sales principle that competitors must overwhelm your criteria in at least a 3:1 ratio to unseat the "First to Engage."

Head-to-Head Strategy: This is the strategy to put into place when you aren't the first to engage. Not surprisingly, the strategy when competing head-to-head is to use that 3:1 ratio.

End Around Strategy: This is "the" strategy to use when what needs to happen is differentiating yourself from the pack.

In football, when the strategy used by the defense is to stop the team with the ball (offense) from gaining yards or a making a touch down is to stop the run up the middle, the team on the defense tends to stack most of their defenders in the middle. To overcome this, the offense often will employ an "End Around" strategy: The quarterback hands to ball off to a wide receiver who then runs around (instead of through) all those stacked up defenders.

Using an End Around strategy for making a presentation usually means selling "higher" in the organization. When you do this you are "running around" and therefore avoiding either lower-level decision influencers or decision makers and/or that pack of competitors presenting to those lower-level decision influencers or decision makers. However, if this is your strategy, you must be completely prepared to present the distinct competitive advantages that not only differentiate you from the pack, put give your competitors no chance of catching up with you before entering the end zone for the touchdown.

Split the Business Strategy: Sometimes you "can win the sale when you don't win the sale." Unlike football, where there's no such thing as "partially" winning a game, if you aren't able to win the total sale, you can then use as a strategy winning a percentage of the sale. The reason why you'd want that to happen is it not only contributes to your revenue, but puts you in a position where you can then develop strategies to take more market share in the future.

Hold Strategy: A hold strategy is used when you discover that you can't meet your prospects needs or solve their problems now – but you will be in the future. What you want to happen is for your customer to "put their buying decision on hold" until your new product, new features, or new services are available.

Do I Know How to Use Effective Presentation Techniques?

You know what type of presentation you'll be giving and your clear on strategy, goals, objectives and tactics. But putting your presentation together can seem daunting. The best place to start when completing a complex task is to break it down into manageable components.

- The Introduction

- The Body

- The Conclusion

- The Q & A

The introduction. The introduction to your presentation is perhaps the most important component because this is when you prospect will develop their "first impression." The most common error is to begin by thanking your prospect for their time, or worse, apologizing for taking it.

Remember asking yourself the question "Would a customer pull out a check book and compensate me just for the sales call?" in our "Top Performers Ask Great Questions" chapter? Your answer needs to be "yes" because, more than anything else, your presentation must not simply communicate value; it must in and of itself create value for your prospect.

This means there is no need to thank your prospect for their time as when your presentation creates real value for your prospect, they'll be thanking you. You can be happy to be there, enthusiastic about the products, solutions, information you're about to impart – but thanking people for their time puts the idea in their head that there is a good possibility you are about to waste their time.

Your introduction is also a great time to share a short (short) anecdote or story about how your company has helped other customers find solutions. You can also provide a brief (brief) summary of your personal experience and expertise, but sharing a short anecdote or story illustrating your personal experience and expertise is usually the better way to go.

The Body. The body is where you offer a logically sequenced, clear, concise, and convincing description of your solution. Be specific and provide concrete examples and whenever possible provide short anecdotal stories that illustrate and/or back up the value of your examples or information. Remember, your presentation is not about you, or even your company. Your presentation is about your prospect. In practice this means making sure every point you make is related to, or referenced by, your prospects unique and specific circumstances, needs, and problems – which you have already carefully researched during the qualifying process.

The Conclusion. Conclusions should always be brief as they highlight the key values your prospect will receive when they buy from you. Conclusions are not the body of your presentation restated.

Once you've summarized key values to your customer, the "conclusion of your conclusion" is usually the best time to introduce your tactic(s) for gaining commitment.

Again, never thank your prospect for their time or the "opportunity." Thanking prospects for the "opportunity" doesn't communicate to your prospect that their best interests are your primary motivator for creating a relationship. You might as well say "Thanks for giving me your time at no charge to me so I have a chance to sell you something."

The Q & A. If you aren't interested in discovering objections or gaps, start off the Q & A by asking "Does anyone have any questions?" Instead, it is much more effective to start off by asking your prospect an open-ended question relating to one of the key points or values in your presentation as this will naturally lead to more questions being asked. When you specifically "ask for a question" your prospect is less likely to ask a "real" question and instead either attempt to appease your request by asking a generic question, or simply telling you they don't have any questions and ending the meeting.

Q & A is also an excellent time to gain commitment as answering your prospect's questions quite often require their "doing something for you" such as arranging another meeting or providing information.

"Visually Marketing" Your Presentation

Visuals are essential to impactful, effective presentations. 85% of the information that enters our brain for processing comes by way of our eyes. This means providing visual images within your presentation is integral to your success. Images can be pictures, diagrams, or graphs – but studies have shown that pictures of people are most effective. But not just any people. For instance, if your text is about software you don't want to use an image of someone tanning on the beach (unless of course you are injecting a little humor, which can also be a good way to get people's attention as well as make the information more memorable to your prospect).

If you are making a PowerPoint presentation, remember that your eyes interpret text as an "image" as well – make good use of bulleting and numbering to simplify information. Be careful not to overwhelm your prospect with too many images at one time or crowd the slide with too much text.

Uniformity and color are also important. A general rule of

thumb is not to use more than three different types of font and keep to three colors. There is a whole science to color; however, generally speaking sticking with your company's logo colors is usually your best bet.

The Narrative of Your Presentation

People remember 20% of what they hear, 30% of what they see, and 50% of what they see and hear. This means that the most powerful way to narrate your presentation is to match what you are saying with what you're prospect is looking at. Using a conversational tone and modulating the volume of your voice (slightly decreasing or increasing for emphasis) also contributes to keeping your prospect's attention as well as promoting their ability to recall information.

If you're presenting to a group, while giving your narrative establish eye contact at different times with different individuals. This lets your individual "audience" members feel that you know they are there, value what they think, and are speaking directly to them. If the group is large, divide it into three sections and then periodically establish eye contact with individuals in each section.

Satisfying the Buying Criteria in Your Presentation

If you are making a Solution Presentation you already know you've earned the right and qualified the customer – which means you should have ascertained your prospect's buying criteria (if not completely, at least to the extent you will now be able to devise questions to elicit specifics of buying criteria). Even if you are making an "Introduction to My Company" presentation you will have garnered buying criteria during the qualifying process. In both types of presentations, your theme needs to be connecting that buying criteria to your solution.

Your presentation is also a good time to review and confirm your research (as well as any conclusions you've made from that research) about your prospect's company and their industry. This confirmation process can lead to your prospect revealing further details regarding buying criteria, as well as uncover gaps and better define urgency.

The End is the Beginning

We started this chapter off with some crazy idea that rock climbing can teach you a lot about sales. Rock climbers know they have to follow a process that works and can be duplicated repeatedly. They have to have specific processes for specific circumstances and in different environments. Most of all they need a process that consistently works because they consistently need to do things right in order not to fall.

We connected the rocks by stating that sales professionals also need to engage in a process that can be duplicated and, when consistently performed, consistently produce the results top performers seek (winning more sales).

But there's another similarity between rock climbers and sales professionals.

Both successful rock climbers and top performing sales professionals are passionate about what they are doing – so passionate that making a single climb or winning a single sale, while celebrated, are never enough.

Winning the sale is never enough. It is just the beginning of the next climb.

Post Chapter Exercise:

1. List the 5 presentation strategies. Why would you choose each one?

2. What is the goal of any presentation?

3. Can you develop a pre-presentation checklist for consistency?

4. Why do prospects say "no?"

5. List your sales call objectives prior to making your next call.

ENGAGEMENT

Where do we go from here?

So, here we are. You get it – you've got to have a process and a plan in place to follow that process. Throughout this book we've emphasized (over and over again) the importance of planning and process. No matter how fired up you are to succeed, no matter how motivated, it is planning and process that drives performance.

No process, no plan – no continuously improving success rate. Period.

In our chapter on the presentation process, we compared sales to rock climbing. We said that you'd better have planned your route, but that the most important part

Step # 5

Approach

Discovery

Vision & Implication

Solution

Engagement

of getting to where you planned to be was to know where you've been. That seemed to make a lot of sense at the time. But that advice might not seem to be as applicable once you've made that presentation and face perhaps the most fragile point in the sales process, the "Golden Moment of Silence" – the point at which you just might feel you've reached the "end of the rope" on your climb to winning the sale.

It is common to refer to this juncture in the process as the point at which we do, or do not, "close" the sale. When we look back on our process we know that we approached our prospect in ways that earned us the right to be where we're at right now. We worked hard to establish our credibility and reliability because we understand that business is not built by "making sales", business is built by building trust. We earned the right to be here now as our goal wasn't "closing the sale" but to become our customer's Trusted Advisor.

We took time to accurately qualify our customer because doing so is in our best interest and the best interest of our customer. We know trust-based professional sales requires investment on the part of all parties involved in the transaction. Investments of value are investments that provide a positive return, so we took the time needed, asked great questions, and in that process provided our customer with the answer to the most important question of all "Why should I buy from you?" by presenting solutions as well as establishing and then satisfying our customer's buying criteria.

The "Golden Moment of Silence" is silent only because we can't hear what our customer is thinking. And you might be surprised to learn that your customer is asking themselves the very same question on your mind, "Where do we go from here?"

So, while you may have thought you were at the end of your rope, the reality is that you are simply at the next stage in your sales process: Engaging the customer by gaining commitment.

You Get What You Ask For

Let's take a look at the word "engage." When we engage in a conversation we participate in that conversation. When we are engaged in an activity we are "doing something." When we place an engagement on our schedule we make a time commitment. So, the word "engage" actually provides us some really great hints as to how to answer the question "Where do we go from here?"

- Participation

- Activity

- Commitment

If we don't receive an immediate commitment from our customer after making our well-prepared presentation (notice I refrained from using the word "close") it is because we have not fully engaged the customer to participate in the sale by performing the activity that fulfills our primary objective. For example, if the primary goal is to win the sale, full participation of the customer means committing to the activity of "getting a check cut."

You'll remember that I already noted we all know "closing" commonly refers to winning the sale. The word "close" infers concepts such as "end" or "stop". We need to be very clear that trust-based sales don't end. You are never finished when it comes to maintaining your role as your customer's Trusted Advisor. What you do close are specific opportunities to win a sale. And when that doesn't translate into winning the sale, this is done by gaining commitment from your customer, and you gain commitment by asking the customer to participate in a meaningful activity that moves the sale forward.

But let's not put the cart before the horse. Untold sales aren't won simply because the opportunity is incorrectly identified as "lost" when all the customer needed in order to fully engage was having a few (and usually relatively minor) details cleared up and/or misconceptions of your offering clarified.

The Object is Winning the Sale

The title for this section aptly demonstrates why it might be we too often close doors customers are actually holding open for us. Even novice sales professionals have at least heard the term "covering objections" and every professional sales person understands that skill in handling customer objections "makes or breaks" winning the sale. Unfortunately, in our culture, when we think a customer "objects" to something we suggest or a position we take there is a tendency to believe this means the person we're speaking to is in opposition or "against" our suggestion or position.

At worst, this cultural bias often causes us to misperceive a customer's objection as a "no." But objections are most commonly perceived as a threat to winning the sale, and perceived threats evoke our "fight or flight" response. When people (including professional sales people) perceive they are in a situation with someone who presents a threat, they tend to become defensive and the relationship and/or conversation can become adversarial – we stand and "fight." It can also be we close a door on winning a sale prematurely by choosing "flight" as our best option for the sale to "survive".

However, what if we changed the way we interpret the meaning of the word "object"?

The object of making your presentation was to win the sale by presenting a useful offering to your customer. Your customer's object in listening to your presentation is to discover a useful offering. In this sense, covering an "objection" is never adversarial because both the sales professional and customer have a shared objective.

Certainly not every prospect you present an offering to will fully engage and commit to the sale. But top performing sales professionals consistently include in their process regularly and accurately confirming a prospect remains highly qualified. If you've done the work, you'll rarely find yourself presenting to a prospect prematurely – but it does happen. Even when in front of a customer ready to buy you will need to cover objections – and this is a continuation of the ongoing process of reconfirming your prospect as highly qualified.

Answering versus Covering Objections

Because you share the same objective as your prospect, you never need to become discouraged or fearful when an objection arises after making your offering. We spent quite a bit of time ridding ourselves of the negative adversarial notions associated with objections. Now let's add to the mix the notion of "covering" something infers the goal of "obscuring" which is the antithesis of our goal in covering objections.

Objections allow us the opportunity to make things clear rather than "cover them up." For example, objections are an opportunity to identify gaps in your offering or in the information the customer provided. Objections are an opportunity to re-enforce your solution. Objections provide further opportunity to build trust.

When you cover an objection, what you are really doing is answering a question. Any objection, even when not made in the form of a question, can be restated as a question. For example, a customer may object by stating that they've worked with the same vendor for years and don't want to risk working with a new company. What that customer is asking is more likely along the lines of "Can your company/product/service ramp up quickly enough to meet our needs?" And that's a question you can answer.

Uncovering Objections

After all this talk about covering versus answering objections, it is rather ironic that, in order to answer an objection; quite often you must first "uncover" the objection. This is done through the process of closing the opportunity.

The steps for successfully closing the opportunity are simple and, again these steps represent a process for closing the opportunity. This is important because, as you'll remember, a process is something that can be learned and duplicated. It is also important because this is the component within the entire sales process that many sales professionals commonly find the most difficult to master. Having a process means that the skills for successfully closing an opportunity can be practiced and mastered.

As you close the presentation:

• State the solution and test the customer's commitment with a solution question.

• Use your customer's answer to identify existing objections.

• Answer objections (i.e. connect to your solution and/or competitive advantage)

• Evaluate your customer's verbal and nonverbal cues (i.e. if the customer is eager to implement, ask for the order now).

• If any objections remain open, answer them.

• If your prospect is not ready to implement than gain commitment from the customer by asking them to commit to an activity that moves the sale forward.

Winning Techniques for Answering Objections

Answering objections is both a skill and a process – a skill that can be learned and a process that can be duplicated. While the process is simple, skill comes when we practice successful techniques:

- Listen without interruption

- Confirm by restating

- Qualify it as the only true objection

- Clarify the objection

- Answer the objection

- Check and test your answer (i.e. ask a great question)

- Ask for commitment

Depending on the complexity of the sale, this process may have to be repeated more than once. It can be helpful to think of the process as wringing out a dishcloth. When you can't squeeze any more water out that cloth, you know you're either ready to ask for the order or ask the customer to commit to an activity that moves the sale forward.

Know What Not to Do

Knowing what not to do is equally as important as knowing what to do. Answering objections can be tricky. Sales professionals and prospects are human beings and this means that emotions and personality are in play.

• Never argue. Even when you're right. Repeat: Never argue.

• Never make a personal attack on your customer or any other person involved in the transaction (i.e. your competition). You can acknowledge a problem or challenge, but never make it personal.

• Never assume you understand what someone means when they use a word and then don't specify how that word applies (i.e. "Could you explain to me what you mean by the word 'complicated'?")

• Never avoid an issue.

• Listen patiently, even if the prospect is angry and/or frustrated.

• Accept responsibility. Never shift responsibility in an attempt to "look better." You won't. Instead, you'll appear irresponsible and unreliable.

• Never make someone "wrong." Educate versus embarrass or insult.

• Never contradict the prospect. It can be quite tempting to do so. Instead, acknowledge their comments and then move on.

• Once you've answered an objection – keep moving forward. Don't dwell.

• Never "guess." If you don't know, say so and then commit to providing an answer.

The Easy Ask

Historically "The Ask" has been the most difficult and challenging step in the sales process for many sales professionals. Why? The answer is really pretty simple: Sometimes we don't ask because, deep down, we really don't want to know. After all, knowing we didn't make the sale means we failed to make the sale. It is a rare profession that success or failure is quite as evident as it is in sales.

Hopefully after reading this book you will have redefined "success." For instance, the ability to accurately identify high quality leads and stop wasting your time on going nowhere deals means you've successfully stopped wasting your time (as well as your customer's) AND will successfully win more sales and exceed more quotas by working with clients who are ready to buy.

However, no matter how successful you are qualifying customers, making the ask remains critical. But just because something is critical doesn't mean it has to be painful. A simple, "Where do we go from here?" will do. True, this very simple question doesn't guarantee you'll get the answer you want to hear, but it will provide you with the answer you need to hear in order to know if the sale is moving forward.

Of course not every prospect will answer this question with "Where do I sign?" Complicated, complex sales cycles by definition mean you can expect to make many "easy asks" and those asks will more often be asking the prospect to commit to engaging in an activity that moves the sale the forward. As a matter-of-fact, you should never leave a sales call without asking for, and then getting, that commitment.

We've established that answering an objection isn't adversarial as the sales professional and prospect have a shared objective. When your prospect is unwilling to commit to doing something that moves the sale forward, it indicates that they do not see continuing the transaction to be of mutual benefit. In other words, you don't share an objective that you are both working to achieve.

But just being able to get a prospect to "do something" doesn't mean they remain committed to working to find a solution or offering from you. The "something" must be specific and meaningful to moving the process forward. For instance, there is a huge difference between networking with a prospect and gaining commitment from a prospect.

A prospect ending the conversation after you've made a presentation by acknowledging they look forward to seeing you at next week's conference or professional gathering is not gaining commitment. A prospect agreeing to meet with you at next week's conference for the purpose of introducing you to a decision influencer does indicate they remain engaged and committed to moving the sale forward.

Commitment: Don't leave the sales call without it.

Sales is a Contact Sport! ™

Post Chapter Exercise:

1. List your top engagement questions:
2. What is a winning technique for answering an objection?
3. What is the goal of closing a sales presentation?

CLOSING THOUGHTS

I am truly fortunate and thankful to have had great teachers and mentors. One of my favorites, Mr. Woods, is a 70 year old business owner who still has a tremendous amount of passion to create and serve others through business.

Mr. Woods encouraged me during a business development strategy session with his organization to remind small business owners and sales professionals there are two business principles that trump all others:

1. "Nothing happens in your business until a sell is made."
2. "It doesn't count as a sales call unless the person you're calling on has the power to say - yes." (fiat power)

Good selling is a noble profession, honorably rooted in trust.

There has been much rhetoric lately about the evil of business and those who create and selling specifically. Many business people are ashamed of the noble profession of selling due to a small segment of individuals.

Selling is honorable. Who teaches physicians about new life saving technologies? Sales people. Who introduces technologies to the world that improve our lives? Sales people. Who offers products to protect our homes, families, and assets? Sales people. You, as a business owner, serve your company as the Chief Sales Officer. Lead from the front.

It's time to change the stereotype and recognize the essential role of sales and respect the men and women who do a difficult and important job well.

Wishing You The Best!

Bruce

5 BONUS RESOURCES

I. Business Strategy Plan Template

Purpose

The purpose of this tool is to help you develop a business strategy plan. It is highly recommended best practice to consult with a sales coach during this process.

How to Use this Template

Complete the following sections with your key stakeholders.

Title Page

[Insert Company Name or Logo]

Business Strategy Plan

[Insert Completion Date]

Table of Contents

4. Strategic Objectives & Key Performance Indicators

   4.1 High-Level Business Objectives

   4.2 Key Performance Indicators

   4.3 GAP Analysis Results

   4.4 Key Success Factors

5. Goals, Measures, Targets, & Initiatives

5.1 Balanced Scorecard Strategy Map

5.2 Brand Scorecard

5.3 Prioritized List of Programs & Projects

5.4 Program Deployment Schedule

1. Executive Summary

1.1 What are the Strategic Objectives and Key Programs for 20xx?

Provide a brief description strategic objectives and key programs that your organization will be implementing over the next 12-18 months.

2. Internal Analysis

2.1 Core Competencies Benchmark

Insert Core Competencies Assessment results and outline areas for improvement.

2.2 Corporate Capabilities & Constraints

Compile & Insert SWOT Analysis results from each department.

2.3 Employee Satisfaction Survey Results

Insert Employee Satisfaction Survey results to demonstrate high staff morale.

3. External Analysis

3.1 Customer Profiles & Market Segments

Insert Customer Profiles results to illustrate profitable customers & market segments.

3.2 Competitive Analysis

Insert Competitive Analysis results to document competitive advantages.

3.3 Product/Service Positioning

Insert Product Positioning Tool results to document current positioning in market.

3.4 Market Conditions & Key Opportunities

Insert STEP Industry Analysis results to highlight market opportunities, threats, conditions, and trends.

4. Strategic Objectives & Key Performance Indicators

4.1 High-Level Business Objectives

Use our Business Objectives Matrix if you need help with ideas.

2012 Business Objectives (examples)

1. Cut operating costs by 25% by end of Q2 2012.
2. Increase New Business Revenue by 15% over last year by end of fiscal year.
3. Revitalize Brand and deploy New Website by end of Q3 2012.
4. Improve Key Performance Indicators in each department by end of 2012.
5. Implement Dashboard to Provide Visibility by end of Q3 2012.

4.2 Key Performance Indicators

Insert Key Performance Indicators for measuring performance in each department.

4.3 GAP Analysis Results

Insert your GAP Analysis to provide a roadmap for improving core competencies.

4.4 Key Success Factors

Insert your Key Success Factors to highlight risks that need to be mitigated.

5. Goals, Measures, Targets, & Initiatives

5.1 Balanced Scorecard Strategy Map

Insert your Balanced Scorecard Strategy Map to document objectives, measures, targets, & initiatives for Financial, Customer, Learning & Growth, and Business Process.

5.2 Brand Scorecard

Insert your Brand Scorecard containing brand objectives, targets, & measures.

5.3 Prioritized List of Programs & Projects

Insert your Priority Index containing all programs & projects. Be sure to organize this list of programs & project by department.

5.4 Program Deployment Schedule

Following is a sample project schedule that you can customize further:

Program Name (examples)	Timeframe
1. Implement CRM System	Q1 20xx– Q3 20xx
2. New Multi-Channel Marketing Campaign	Q2 20xx – Q4 20xx
3. Redesign Corporate Website	Q1 20xx – Q3 20xx

4. Update Policies & Procedures   Q1 20xx
5. Introduce Products to EMEA   Q2 20xx
Marketplace

II. Sales Support Checklist

Purpose

The purpose of this tool is to provide a checklist for improving sales support.

Sales Support Checklist

Done	Description of Task	Completed	Notes
	Sales Skills Assessments complete		
	Sales Training Manual complete		
	Sales Script standardized		
	Feature, Advantage, Benefit Tool built and distributed to sales staff		
	Competitive Analysis complete		

Objection Response Tool
distributed

Opportunity Pipeline Tool is
used

Sales Proposal standardized

Key Account Plan exercise
complete

Case Study exercise
completed

Sales Process Established

Sales Presentation
standardized

Individual Goals being
documented

Pricing Sheet, Whitepapers,
FAQ, and other marketing
collateral updated

Advanced CRM training
completed

III. **Sales Management Checklist**

Purpose

This tool is to provide a checklist for managing sales territories. Implementing a strategic sales territory management process will reduce travel time & expenses, increase health of your account base, and help to generate more sales.

Territory Management Checklist

Done	Description of Task
	Analyze Territory Sales from Last Year – Sales Analysis Tool
	Identify your Annual Sales Target for New & Renewal Business
	Determine amount of product/service sales required to achieve sales target
	Use Closing Ratios to determine # prospects required to achieve sales target

Identify # daily cold calls required to generate required # prospects for target

Evaluate Key Accounts and Create Action Plan for each key account

Profile Customers to understand revenue potential for different account types

Complete Account Scoring exercise to benchmark health of account base

Quadrant Your Territory – Ensure equidistance from Home Base (office)

Evaluate Territory Management Software Tools with Sales Management

Select a Home Base (office) that is central to each of your 4 quadrants

Create Sales Proposal, Sales Script, Sales Call Report, & Sales Presentation

Develop Sales Opportunity Pipeline Report to provide increased visibility

Create Prospects List for all prospective organizations in your territory

Schedule your Days – Cold Calling, Sales Calls, Proposals, Internal Meetings

Schedule Territory Days – use rolling 4-day schedule to develop quadrants

IV. **Individual Goals Template**

Purpose

This tool is to help you document your individual goals, deliverables, timelines, and how results will be measured.

Best Practices

Use the simple SMART goal-setting heuristic:

S – Specific

M – Measurable

A – Actionable

R – Realistic

T – Time-Sensitive

Ensure that each of your goals are reviewed to include the following:

- Goal Description
- Value Created
- Deliverables

- Deadlines
- Metrics & Measures

Organizational Goals & Objectives

Briefly outline individual key goals & objectives for this fiscal year.

1. Mountain Top Goal #1
2. Mountain Top Goal #2
3. Mountain Top Goal #3

Personal Vision Statement

Work to create a strategic vision statement. What is it you would specifically like to achieve in your career?

Individual Goals

List each of the specific goals you would like to set for yourself.

1. Goal #1

Description of Goal:

Value Created by Achieving this Goal:

Deliverables:

- <Deliverable 1>
- <Deliverable 2>

Deadlines:

- <Date for deliverable 1>
- <Date for deliverable 2>

Success of this Goal will be measured by:

2. Goal #2

Description of Goal:

Value Created by Achieving this Goal:

Deliverables:

- <Deliverable 1>
- <Deliverable 2>

Deadlines:

- <Date for deliverable 1>
- <Date for deliverable 2>

Success of this Goal will be measured by:

3. Goal #3

Description of Goal:

Value Created by Achieving this Goal:

Deliverables:

- <Deliverable 1>

- <Deliverable 2>

Deadlines:

- <Date for deliverable 1>

- <Date for deliverable 2>

Success of this Goal will be measured by:

V. SWOT Analysis Tool

Purpose

The purpose of this tool is to provide assistance with evaluating your Strengths, Weaknesses, Opportunities, and Threats. Strengths & weaknesses are generally INTERNAL, while opportunities & threats are normally EXTERNAL.

Strengths	Weaknesses
• Robust Product Knowledge	• Lack of Competitive Data
•	•

Opportunities	Threats
• Cross-selling new products	• Data vulnerable to virus
•	•

Works Cited & Great Resources

Adamson, M. D. (2011). *The Challenger Sale*. New York: Penguin Group.

Gitomer, J. (2003). *The Sales Bible*. New Jersey: John Wiley & Sons.

Jordan, J. (2012). *Cracking The Sales Management Code*. New York: McGraw Hill Companies.

Maister, D. (1997). *The Trusted Advisor*. New York: The Free Press.

Michelli, J. A. (2012). *The Zappos Experience*. 2012: The McGraw Hill Companies.

Miller, M. (2010). *A Seat at the Table*. Austin: Greenleaf Book Group Press.

Riggs, K. S. (2008). *1-on-1 Management: What Every Great Manager Knows That You Don't*. P3 Press.

Sellers, M. (2007). *The Funnel Principle*.

Smith, J. L. (2006). *Creating Competitive Advantage*. New York: Doubleday.

Webb, M. J. (2006). *Sales and Marketing Six Sigma Way*. New York: Kaplan Publishing.

Wilson, L. W. (1998). *Play To Win: Choosing Growth Over Fear in Work and Life*. New York: Bard Press.

Jim Collins, Jerry I. Porras (2002)*Built to Last: Successful Habits of Visionary Companies* (Harper Business Essentials)

INDEX

Notes:

Notes:

Notes:

Made in the USA
Charleston, SC
04 February 2013